The Dating Game

Insights Into Affairs of The Heart

Brigid Bishop

The Dating Game

The Dating Game

Author's Preface

The Dating Game, Insights Into Affairs of the Heart, is a collection of blogs that I produced during the course of my New Age Life Coaching practice in an attempt to drive certain key points home to my client base.

Repeatedly, certain themes and issues come up with clients, and so, in an attempt to assist clients in overcoming insecurities and codependency, I have assembled these blogs into this book.

Relationship Coaching at your finger tips, so to speak.

Some of these blogs are intentionally written with a "tongue in cheek" attitude, but the majority of them are sincere and are meant to assist the reader in achieving their relationship goals, whatever they may be.

I hope that you gain some useful insight into your own relationship style by reading this book, and I also hope that you can better position yourself for healthy relationships by doing so.

Thank you.

Brigid Bishop

Dedication

I would like to dedicate this book to all of the people that I have had relationships with during my life, whether positive or negative, as you have helped make me what I am today. Without the experiences that we shared I would not have been able to write this book, which, for the most part, is based on my own personal relationship history.

Thank you.

Brigid Bishop

The Dating Game

Table of Contents

Chapter One

The Search For Love

The Dating Game

The Dating Game

You Are Who You Meet!

Yes, it's true, you ARE who you Meet.

You're thinking, "Wait a minute Brigid, you mean that all these jerks I'm meeting are me?"

Sadly, if the quality of the people that you are meeting and allowing into your life is not high, then, yes, they are mirroring your self-image and the old sayings of our mother's "like attracts like" and "birds of a feather flock together" are true.

Ok, so now your adrenalin is a bit "up" and your face is red, and you're thinking "this woman doesn't know what she's talking about".

Take a deep breath.

There.

Now read on and see if you can grasp the concept I am putting forth to you.

Maybe you are meeting a lot of high quality people, people who are caring, responsible, relationship-ready….then this blog is not for you. You already have enough self-respect and self-confidence to attract your mirror images and you will have some healthy choices to select from. It is highly likely that you are not in need of a Tarot Reading, unless it is just to do a little spot check to see how things look to develop. You are not my target audience.

If, on the other hand the men that you are meeting are self-centered, fear commitment, erratic, irresponsible, inconsistent in communication, or even worse, non-communicative, then you are my target audience. You are even more part of this audience if you are already perceiving yourself in *some sort of relationship* but can't define it because it is in limbo. The reasons the relationship remains in limbo are very likely some combination of the aforementioned personality traits.

So, you view yourself as responsible, commitment-ready, stable, a good communicator, but the people who are stumbling into your life are not.......what does this mean????

You have no one to blame but yourself.

OOOOHHHH! Another adrenalin rush.

Take a breath, a deep one.

Read ON.....

People will behave in self-centered and inconsiderate ways to you only when you ALLOW them to.

What????

Yes. You are setting a precedent and condoning the poor treatment you may be receiving each and every time you accept these types of behaviors. You must learn to *reject any and all unacceptable behaviors* on the part of any one individual you allow into your life, whether it is a lover, a friend, a coworker, whomever, but most especially any one individual that you are considering having a romantic relationship with.

Love relationships *only work when there is true respect and trust* between the two people.

If you are always second guessing your partner's next move, if you never feel secure about whether he's going to call when he says he will, you are already on a slippery slope to Deadendville. You feel insecure about his calling because the last time he said he'd call during the week, he didn't, and you got antsy and called him on Thursday and he cut it short and didn't call you until the following Monday....

The Dating Game

This is **unacceptable behavior** on the part of the person you have allowed into your life.

What to do?

You cannot control the other person.

The only thing you **can control is yourself!!**

So what do you do when he doesn't call as he said he would?

NOTHING!!!

You simply **REJECT THE UNACCEPTABLE BEHAVIOUR!**

What does that mean?

It means that you do not allow people to treat you in disrespectful or neglectful ways. You never chase after someone whom is not giving you proper attention, you withdraw from the situation. By withdrawing you are giving them a very **clear message** that if they expect to have a **chance of being part of your world they must treat you with respect.**

You are who you meet. It is as simple as that. Demand to be treated well. If you receive anything less, reject it! Don't expect to receive proper treatment from a person who thinks that you are always available at their beck and call. These types of people will always take you for granted and will only give you proper attention when **they feel like it.** it won't change by allowing it to continue. The only way it will be changed is by you changing yourself and having the self-respect and self-confidence to say to yourself "I will not tolerate being treated this way, I deserve better, and I **WILL FIND BETTER!"**

If the person in question adjusts and corrects their treatment of you, reward their good behavior by gracing them with your attention, if not, it's no big loss!! They weren't worth your time and don't deserve a great person like you!

YOU ARE WHO YOU MEET! BECOME THE PERSON WHOM OTHERS TREAT WITH DIGNITY AND RESPECT AND THAT IS WHAT YOU WILL ATTRACT!!

Oh, I hear some of you lamenting now "But I love him! I want him! If I don't keep myself on hold for him he will find someone else!"

STOP THAT!

That is not love. Love is a combination of affection, sexual attraction, chemistry, trust and respect and validation of feelings. Sitting around waiting and wondering if he will call while he is out doing his own thing is not going to change things. Getting off your butt and making plans to go out and socialize and meet even more (and potentially BETTER) people will.

Either

    a) The original love interest will realize you are not on hold for him/her anymore and puts forth the proper effort

or

    b) You will meet someone new who starts off right out of the gate giving you the proper attention.

YOU ARE WHO YOU MEET!

The Dating Game

Where Is My John Wayne????

This is a common question on women's' minds, and even more frequently, I pick up the phone and the querent on the other end of the line asks me "*When will someone new come into my life, and where will I meet him?*".

Being a Professional Tarot Reader for nearly seven years, I can tell you of the 20,000+ readings I have provided, that this is one of the most difficult questions to answer.

First of all, _**Timing and the Tarot**_ is very difficult, I can provide you with my best estimate, however, I cannot nail it down to a specific day. Dependent upon how the cards come up in your reading, whether they are very distinctively giving me a clear answer, or kind of misty and weak, giving me an indeterminate answer, is how I can provide an answer for you.

When the cards come up well defined as to when, and the type of man the querent is going to meet it is because the querent is doing all of the free will exercises that she needs to improve her odds of bringing love into her life. This means she is very social, gets out and puts herself in social situations, doesn't sit at home and wait for the new man to somehow *"beam down"* from metaphysical ectoplasm into her living room. These readings are usually extremely accurate and easy for me to interpret.

The difficult reads are the querents who get the weak cards. The opportunities and possibilities are there, but the cards are weak because the querent is living a very asocial existence and is not *"getting out there"*.

I give readings in an honest and forthright manner, and if *I DON'T* see someone new coming in within the time frame I am scouring, I will tell the querent so. If the querent is open to more than just a *"psychic quickie"* and is really looking to change her situation, I will tell her straight out that her cards are telling her she needs to make certain changes. Whether it is taking a class in something she always wanted to learn, joining a club or organization, checking out an online dating service, getting involved in volunteer work, or just doing a little *"clubbing"* with the girls to get herself out there........changes need to be made.

If you are in the same set social pattern and are not meeting anyone to date, you need to **MAKE CHANGES**! Someone new is not going to pop onto the scene if the scene never changes. You have to change the scene!

As far as meeting men at work goes, I highly advise against it, the reason being that if it does not work out, you still have to go to work every day, and hence, may be uncomfortable around the individual in question for the balance of your employ, but I highly recommend taking advantage of meeting men literally **EVERYWHERE ELSE!!!**

Some querents ask me where to go to meet men. *The answer is OUT!* Out to the library, the bookstore, the convenience store around the corner, the pottery class, the local Red Cross to give blood........in traffic, *EVERYWHERE!*

There is no "Magickal Place" where they keep all the men that you need to discover, you just need to open your eyes and look around you.........they are, literally, **EVERYWHERE!!**

The trick is how to turn a casual passing-by into a conversation.

Please read my blog on "An Experiment In Utilizing Your Feminine Energy" and put it into practice! "

You will be meeting your John Wayne and your Marlboro Man everywhere you go, conversing and practicing your receptive energies to perfection........that is what draws men in and that is what motivates them to ask you for your number.

The Dating Game

If you don't want to click over to read the blog, it's this simple......you see a gentleman that appeals to you, **ANYWHERE**, and you do nothing but smile and maintain eye contact with him for ten full seconds, count them off.........you will have more spontaneous conversations than you can count!

A lot of women respond to me with ***"Oh, I signed up for a class, and it was filled with women".*** So what? On your travel to the class, you have multiple opportunities, in class, the women you so disdainfully matriculate with have brothers and single friends that you could meet if you took the time to befriend them a bit.

Volunteer organizations like the American Red Cross (*of which I am a member*) are a fantastic way to meet multitudes of people, and people know people, the more people you meet, the larger your network, and the wider the net you cast.

My answer on where to meet men is: ***Everywhere!***

Top Ten Ways to Stay Single For Life

I was once told that successful blogging is inclusive of providing your audience with lists, so, not one to avoid testing a theory, I decided to post this list for my blog audience and clients to peruse.

It may be a bit *"Tongue in Cheek"*, but I can tell you, it will work for you!

#1 Find yourself an unavailable man, i.e., married, emotionally unavailable, noncommittal, workaholic, alcoholic or otherwise occupied. Decide he is the only one for you, put your entire life on hold waiting for him to give up his marriage, his girlfriend, his second job, his booze, his drugs, or whatever his particular obsession may be.

#2 When you are online dating, stop looking as soon as you meet one guy in person and focus all of your energy and attention on him, put your life on hold waiting for his next call, your next date, his next text message or email and then, when he moves on, repeat the process repeatedly.

#3 ALWAYS be available for his calls, texts and emails, never close your IM window so you know when he logs in and out and stalk him on the net watching his every move, neglect your own social life and worry about his. Respond immediately each and every time he makes contact.

#4 When he doesn't call you in a timely manner make every excuse in the book as to why he is not communicating with you for him, his job, his kids, his hobby, they are all taking up his time and he will call you eventually, sit by the phone and wait.

#5 Panic if one day goes by and he doesn't call you. Do not let twenty-four hours go by without communication, immediately pick up your phone and call or text him, email him, forward him those annoying group emails to see if he opens it, repeat in increasing frequencies when he does not answer his phone and you get voicemail.

#6 Convince yourself that you are in a relationship that does not exist. He smiles at you when you pass in the hall at work, begin obsessing that he is going to ask you out and focus all of your energy into making your work day revolve around his desk, heck, transfer departments if it gives you the office next to his.

#7 Convince yourself that a casual dating situation is a real relationship. He doesn't call you more than once every ten days or so, you only see him once or twice a month, but heck, he's busy with his kids, job, business, hobby, etc., see reason #4.

#8 Chase him! Go where you know he will be. Show up with friends as if you were going there anyway and spend all of your time trying to get his attention and get him into your social group, ignore your friends, they were just "the beard" anyway.

#9 Be overly critical. You are at a party where you don't know too many people, just mildly acquainted, they seem to be his friends, he is off socializing and had you on his arm, but you wanted his undivided attention so you went off to sit on the sofa alone. In front of all of his friends, tell him how rude he is to ignore you and have the nerve to socialize with other people and assume that he was including you.

#10 Be a total narcissist. Analyze how each and every action he takes affects you. He's going to visit his mother on your cat's birthday? How dare he, doesn't he know how important that cat is to you. His mother is dying and he has to spend time sharing shifts with his siblings caring for her? How dare he! Doesn't he know that you need to go out to dinner and a movie tonight! He spends time with his friends. How dare he! Doesn't he know that YOU are the only friend he needs? Make sure you tell him all of these things every time he takes a breath that does not include you or calculate how it will affect you.

So, my dear friends, here is a handy guide to the Top Ten Ways to Stay Single for Life.

There are many more ways, but these are just the best ways. Even applying just one of these will give you some pretty heavy insurance that you will never have to deal with that messy thing called a "Relationship".

The One, The Myth Exposed

The **ONE**

Are We Meant To Be Together?

This question, more than any other question that is asked of me, this question makes me very tense. It bothers me because I do not subscribe to the idea or fantasy that there exists out there "The One".

In my personal belief system, I just cannot buy into this particular myth.

Some people believe that a "**Soul Mate**" is "**The One**", ugh, it rattles my cage when I hear or read people encouraging this fantasy in others.

This mindset leads people to pursuing relationships that won't work and to holding on to relationships that don't work, and frequently gets them obsessed with an ex.

There is no such thing as "**The One**". The Universe is not so cruel as to, in the 6,709,999,582 people who are on the earth, (as of 7/1/08), to only have **ONE** of these people be an appropriate loving and caring partner for **YOU**.

Statistically, if you were born on 7/1/08, that would give you a **0.00000001490313058561980000% Chance of finding someone to love!**

Do you really believe that the odds are stacked that overwhelmingly against us here on Earth?

I don't.

I believe that we have dozens, perhaps hundreds or thousands, of mortal counterparts that we can build a happy existence with. Fate plays a hand to some degree. Yes, fate being the geographic location of your existence, the personality you were born with, (**whether you are** *an introvert or extrovert*), the genetics that compose your outward appearance, how your parents raised you and thus how you are wired emotionally and psychologically and more, but I vehemently disregard that fate controls "who we are meant to be with".

We **CHOOSE** who we are with (*or not with and pining away after*).

So when a client says this to me, distraught over a crisis in their current love affair, I have no choice but to say, "I cannot in good conscience answer that question as there is no such thing as "The ONE"". This statement is frequently met with dead silence.

Yes, there may be a soul connection to this individual you love so much, yes, they may even be your "*Soul Mate*", but they are NOT the only "*ONE*" and it is not "*Meant To BE*" you must choose to **MAKE IT BE**! And to top that off, they must also decide, hopefully concurrently, that they want you to be **THEIR ONE**.

So your relationship is in crisis, you don't know if it is over, you are looking for relief. The easiest question to ask is "Are we meant to be together?" It will provide you with instant validation and relief if an advisor tells you "yes, you are", and drive you perhaps to despair if an advisor answers "No, you are not."

Better questions to ask are "What can I do (if anything) to improve the situation", or "What are the core issues and root causes of our relationship issues", or "What do I need to work on internally to better cope with this crisis".

These are questions that can be answered with true advice that can help you to better choose as to whether or not this individual truly is right for you and deserves to be in the "*ONE*" position in your life, rather than just trying to validate that your suffering will be worth it in the long run.

So if you do call me, and you do ask me, "Are we meant to be together, is he/she the one?" I will tell you, again, I cannot in good conscience answer that question as I do not believe that there is any such thing as "***The One***".

Do the Math!!!!

The Dating Game

I get this **over and over and over again** in my professional practice. Women, who are otherwise **intelligent** and **logical** beings become irrational and unrealistic and anxiety ridden when the object of their affections becomes ambivalent, or worse, uninterested.

I am not talking about those in "long term" relationships. I am talking about those who are truly single and dating who don't want to give a relationship time to grow or develop naturally, or don't allow the male to take the "reins" so to speak, of the masculine energy role (the initiator) and jump the gun in oh so many ways.

The advice that I give over and over and over again, which **VERY few follow**, is to remove their energy and attention **AWAY** from the gentleman who is behaving in a distant manner. This means, don't call him up, don't text him, don't stalk him online, don't invite him out..........the female (at the dating stage) must allow the male the time and the "room" to decide whether or not he wants to take this further, which is not on the same schedule as the female.

Females tend to decide very quickly that they want to be involved. They may have just flirted with a gentleman and they will call me and ask "is this the guy that I am going to marry". Although the cards will show if there is a **POTENTIAL** for a long term relationship, if you have just met a guy this weekend and he hasn't even asked you out yet, this question is based on suppositions galore and it is not likely that you will get a very accurate answer.

Tarot Readings are not set in stone. They will tell you what is **LIKELY** to happen if you remain on the same path, continue with the same types of actions, into the future. Any changes in YOUR behavior change the outcomes of the situation...Tarot Readings are a living, breathing, metaphysical wonder and change as your actions change.

A more apropos question at the first stages of infatuation would be "will he ask me out" and then after a date or so "will we develop a relationship" perhaps after 6-9 months of exclusive dating...."will he consider marrying me".......the questions have to be realistic in comparison to the situation in order to have any sense of accuracy.

If you want to be the "feminine" energy in a relationship with a "masculine" male, as archaic as it may sound, you must allow him to set the pace. If it is not in your nature to allow this, then you may be a *"masculine" energy female*, or if you are truly *"feminine" energy*, you need to discipline yourself to your natural energy.

All modern women must maintain a masculine energy at work, and our "go get it if you want it" attitude will serve us well in our careers, but **NOT** in our relationships (unless he is a feminine energy male), but this post is about the majority....we shall discuss the opposing roles later.

Ok, so he is a masculine energy male. He wants to be **TRUSTED**. He wants you to think he is **COMPETENT**. So why would you pick up the phone and call him and ask him out for the weekend??? It makes him feel like you are taking the lead and that you do not feel he is man enough, or responsible enough to be able to ask YOU out. He may say yes, but you are setting a playing field where you will ultimately lose!

Your role, as the feminine energy, is to *ACCEPT or REJECT* whatever this man presents to you. If he does not call you within a comfortable amount of time, it doesn't mean you call him and take the lead, it means you *REJECT* his negligence and busy yourself with friends or on other dates with males who respect you enough to follow up with you.

If a male tells you he would rather "be friends", it does not mean that he really down deep wants to be your lover but is afraid of commitment, or was hurt and afraid he will be hurt again. It means he **IS NOT** interested in being your lover...move on. If he changes his mind, he will be back.

The most effective means of measuring a man's interest is to keep moving on, keep moving forward **UNTIL HE ASKS YOU** to stop, stay still with him for awhile.

The Dating Game

Until a man asks you to be exclusive to him **DATE YOUR BUTT OFF!!!** If you are in a dating slump......keep yourself busy doing the things you've always wanted to do....live your life as you imagine in your mind......start living the life you imagine.....on your own!!!!

Nothing draws a man out more than the absence of your energy. If you allow him to feel your absence, he will feel the need to connect, and *he will INITIATE*!!! If you are always there, texting him, phoning him, lurking on line, he has *NO MOTIVATION* to connect...........you are always available...so there is no sense of urgency for him to get some of your time and attention...he already has it!!!

The Dating Game Continues

So, You Are a Masculine Energy Female You Say?

Ok, you've read my views and insights to date on the Feminine Energy female and you see how that works for them, but it's just not you. Although you are truly female through and through, you are a *Masculine Primary Energy Female.*

What does this mean?

It means that you are probably primarily Air or Fire in your natal chart, and there are several other indicators of this primary energy. You are likely to have been first born, or perhaps responsible as a youngster for normally adult duties. You have been the one (all of your life), who takes charge of situations, you know what is best for those you love, you are protective of those you love, you are assertive in your outward actions, you tend to see what you want and go after it, never waiting for it to come to you.

Go Girl!

This is my primary energy, so I understand it well, and know the pitfalls.

Here are some of the issues that a Masculine Energy Female tends to encounter:

a) Being such a strong entity, you believe that you need a strong male, even stronger than you are (i.e. a Masculine Energy Male).

b) Although you have spent a lifetime being strong, you long for someone to let your guard down around.

c) You find yourself frequently in leadership positions, whether you seek to lead or not.

d) You tend to provide for those you love, whether they ask for it or not, sometimes gifting them to death, to show your love. However, when you don't receive to the same degree in return, it stings.

e) AGAIN, you believe you need a Masculine Energy Male in your life and you *frequently pursue this type of male....*

Ok, let's look at your need and longing for a Masculine Energy Male. You have spent your life taking care (quite well, I might add), of yourself and others. You provide materially, economically, emotionally and perhaps spiritually. You protect them. You coach them. You have earned their respect and their trust. You are an icon of strength and reliability to them. You may not have had a strong father figure, and thus, have fathered yourself and those around you, or perhaps you had an extremely strong father figure, and thus, emulated his behavior in preference over your mother's possibly passive behavior.

As adult women, we tend to seek either men who are *identical* to our early father figures, or *the extreme opposite.*

Ok, so the man you want needs to be a good provider in every sense of the word as above, a protector, a coach and confidant, and worthy of your trust and respect. He must be strong and reliable.

You meet such a man.

You pursue him...assertively. You walk up to him, you start the conversation, you initiate the next contact, the masculine male is flattered, and since you are dealing with him on his "masculine" terms, he believes you to be capable of continuing the connection in a very "male" way. Which means, he assumes he already has your trust and respect, he knows you can take care of yourself and therefore feels no need to protect you. He knows you are competent so he feels no need to coach or guide you, and he knows you are strong so there is no need to "coddle" you by courting you as he would a feminine energy female.

The Dating Game

The problem here is, there is no balance. You basically have left no room for nurturing, cherishing or protection to take place, so your relationship itself takes on a masculine energy. The effects tend to be that since you are both operating in masculine mode, he frequently doesn't call, doesn't make plans, doesn't discuss your issues with you for insight (or his), and you end up in extensive waiting periods between interactions, possibly going into "chase" mode, or delaying any opportunity for commitment between you.

In order to achieve that balance, there are only two options for you.

Option One: If you truly "love" this particular masculine energy entity, you must, inject some feminine energy into the relationship. This means practicing your feminine energy skills, going against your *primary energy*, or

Option Two: Accept that you cannot change your *primary energy* and seeking out the companionship of a Feminine Energy Male.

Let's look at Option One. This is the guy, this is the one, you have to have him, he plays Rhett Butler to the Scarlett O'Hara in your mind. This can be done but it is DIFFICULT to say the least. It is retraining yourself in the ways you utilize your personal powers. It means going into waiting mode for contact, not initiating in any way, going into a mode of purely "accepting" or "rejecting" what the Masculine Energy Male presents to you. Rejecting means that when his behavior is unacceptable, you simply let him know that you "don't want to feel this way because he has done a, b, or c". "Accepting" is offering him positive reinforcement for the actions you do enjoy by telling him "I feel so happy (good, comfortable, etc.) when you do a, b, or c", and sitting back and letting him take the reins.

You do not offer him advice, (unless he asks for it), you do not initiate calls or dates, you allow him to set the pace and steer the relationship. In return, you will find that the masculine energy male will feel you "submitting" to his energy and it will bring out the best, most potent masculinity of his nature, providing you with protection from the outside world, guidance, validation of your feelings and cherishment for your feminine nature.

This is all well and good, and as time progresses you will learn to balance out with each other and switch back and forth between your energies, you can allow your masculinity to surface from time to time, etc., as your bond has been formed in balance of the masculine and feminine.

The DANGER here is when you cannot sublimate your masculine energy long enough to achieve balance and you prematurely try to let your natural energy out. If you go along for a month as the feminine energy and then let your masculine energy surface, the male may well feel emasculated and the whole thing can fall to pieces. You have to be patient and assume the feminine energy until you reach the commitment point, projected at around nine months for the average relationship.

The OTHER DANGER is that you may begin to feel emasculated yourself. You may have a PROBLEM giving up that much control and going against your natural energies (I did), and you begin to rebel and take your power back, again, the relationship will fall apart. Examine how hard it would be for you to give up control for a nine-month period, and think it through. If it is not in you to have the patience to balance this out through conscious effort, then Option Two is the better option for you.

If you can do it, you can have a working relationship with the masculine energy male. I did it, and so can you, but it was a long, drawn-out process, and now we are at that happy point of commitment and contentment where we both swing back and forth between our Masculine and Feminine. Problems DO still arise when we are both being Masculine or both being Feminine, and that is when I step back, and temporarily switch my energy mode to achieve balance once again. It takes work. All relationships do, it's just knowing what work needs to be done.

Option two would require you to seek the companionship of a Feminine Energy Male from the get-go.

This does not mean that the man is in any way "effeminate", it means that he is not the assertive, driven, masculine energy male. He is frequently left-handed (right-brained), creative and caring, the sensitive type. He prefers to have his feelings validated, and although he may be successful and an excellent wage earner, he is not good at steering his boat and needs direction in the sea of life. These males are almost always creative in some way. They look for strong women to steer them in the right direction, they want your advice and your input from day one. They want and need a masculine energy to balance out their lives. They are not necessarily "weak", but they are more feeling oriented than action oriented as individuals. These are the men that take well to role-reversal situations, becoming the stay at home parent very easily, supporting their wives' careers very naturally, etc.

With these men you are free to fully embrace your Masculine Female Energy. You initiate everything at the beginning, you take charge, you call the shots (and the man), you make the plans for your future, and this male will succumb to your strength and love and respect you.

I have had Feminine Energy lovers in my life, and I have found that the DANGER here is, when I wanted to switch to the balancing mode during the commitment stage, that I became resentful of having to always be in charge, and needed the male to shoulder the lead for awhile, and that is when I broke the commitments. It did not work out for me, but it may for you.

So, if you have no qualms about primarily taking the lead and the control of your relationship, this will work well for you. You know he is truly a Feminine Energy Male if he responds well to your pursuit of him in the beginning. When you call, he calls you right back. When you ask him out, he accepts readily. When you suggest a dating activity to him, he is eager to attend. When you tell him of your life issues, he doesn't offer you advice and tell you how to fix it like the Masculine Energy Male will, he listens. If you ask for his guidance he will offer it, but, if you don't ask, he will listen and tell you how he knows how you feel, he will validate your feelings rather than guiding you.

And, again, as your reach the commitment stage, out at around nine months, you will switch back and forth with your energies, but your primary, unless practiced, will always show through.

So, if you have any questions or need to take a deeper look at the energies in your relationships, give me a ring and through the use of Tarot, Intuition and Experience, I will assist you in achieving this energy balance.

The Dating Game

Looking for Love? Line Up Your Energy!

Many adult single women are looking to find love, it's the nature of the beast. We long to pair ourselves with someone, to be appreciated, to have a *"special someone"* to share our thoughts and feelings with on a consistent basis and to open ourselves to building a foundation together.

There is absolutely nothing wrong with seeking to love and be loved, however, many women just don't seem to be successful in achieving the relationships that they so strongly desire. Why is that?

Well, there are about as many reasons why a woman can't find love as there are stars in the sky, let's take a hard look at one or two of them in today's blog.

You must define what your primary energy is. Are you passive in nature? Are you able to sit back and simply accept or reject that which a man may offer to you? *If so, you are a primary feminine energy.*

Are you a go-getter in all areas of your life? Are you very extroverted? Do you initiate contact with men you are interested in? *If so, you are a primary masculine energy.*

Ok, so the modern, successful woman meets a man she is interested in and he asks her out. During the beginning of the relationship, at least for the first few weeks, she presents herself as a feminine energy, allowing him to initiate contact and suggest dates, etc., and things seem to go along fairly well for a few weeks or a month or two. What begins to happen, however, is that she wants to *"pick up the pace"* a bit, she's anxious to find love, and this gentleman appears to be a suitable potential mate, and she wants to increase the amount of time they spend together and the frequency of communication.

Now, the unassuming guy, not knowing that she feels this intense need to be loved, *(because she presents herself initially as calm, cool and collected, in no particular hurry to commit to a relationship),* thinks that things are going along just fine when they see each other once or twice a week and communicate once or twice a week. So he doesn't realize that she is already experiencing a level of impatience and wanting more from him than this.

Each time he has called and asked her out, she has been available and accepted, and she had no problems being physical with him at a rather early stage in their "**relationship**", early being defined here as under the two month mark for dating time.

He has no idea that she has already, (**nearly immediately**), stopped dating other men and is focused on **HIM**. Period.

She has unknowingly communicated to him that she has no problem being ultra casual with him, whether she knows it or not.

So the gentleman in question sees no problem when he calls her on Friday evening to get together that same night, (**no advanced planning**), and when he takes her to his place for sex after their **"date"**, he feels no special bond with her, although he likely enjoys the physical pleasure. On Saturday morning they go back into their own separate worlds and he may not contact her again for as long as a week, again, asking for the last minute date, which she readily accepts.

He goes about his business during the week and because he believes the connection to be ultra casual due to the behavior pattern involved, he really doesn't think about her much until he has some free time on his hands and an urge to be physical again.

In the meantime, the woman in question is spending the bulk of her time from Saturday morning until his next call talking to her girlfriends about him, projecting a future for them as a "**couple**" and anxiously waiting for her phone to ring, allowing little else to occupy her thoughts. Typically at this stage I get calls from single clients asking me to read the tarot for them to find out how he **"feels"** about them. This is not an unusual or unrealistic question, but what strikes me time and time again is the women who call generally don't take the time to consider how

THEY feel about **HIM**! Their only concern is whether or not he has feelings for them and whether or not the potential for him to fall in love with them is there. They don't seem to take even a minute of their time to consider whether or not they actually **LIKE** the man in question or feel that they could fall in love with him.

In addition, they tend to keep their weekends open, failing to make plans with friends or date other men, anticipating any predefined **"pattern"** they discern from past experience with the man in question in order to ensure that they are available should he choose to again make last minute contact and spend time with them.

Because they are not continuing to develop other relationships or social activities, they become anxious about **"how things are going", "when will he call"**, etc. and have themselves in a heightened state of anxiety until they hear from the gentleman in question.

Usually, at this stage, is when the woman in question starts destroying any chance of building a relationship with the man. Why? Because they have gotten themselves into a casual sexual affair and they now want to change it into a **"relationship".** So how do they destroy the connection? Oh, there are many varied ways, but these are the most common in my observations.

Odds are, she nearly immediately added him to her network on whatever social networking site she may frequent, such as myspace or facebook, so she is **"keeping an eye"** on him in cyberspace, watching what he posts, what anyone else is posting on his page and keeping tabs on any friends he may add. The addition of any new female immediately creates a state of panic in the woman, and may cause her to add some new **"friends"** of her own to illicit a reaction from him. Highly unlikely to happen as the man in question is unlikely to be paying close attention to her facebook page anyway as he is still considering himself as single and available and behaving as if he is.

When she is unable to illicit a response she may begin posting provocative pictures of herself and perhaps other males **(that she is**

NOT involved with) hoping, again, to illicit some response or reaction from the man in question. Again, this **WILL NOT** happen as he just assumes she is also dating others, after all, he is only calling/seeing her once a week (**or less**), so what she does with the rest of her time is her business.

When passive attempts at gaining his attention fail, she begins to become assertive in her need to gain his attention by emailing, texting and/or calling him, making him feel that she is *"omnipresent"* and pressuring him. This usually results in him cutting conversations short, whether via text, phone or computer IM.

Another way she escalates is, rather than waiting for a call and an invitation for a date, she creates opportunities to be together in advance of his being able to set something up. She begins to initiate the contact, invite him to parties she is throwing, **(that she would not be hosting except to make a reason for him to spend time with her),** attend movies or sporting events that she believes will interest him and so forth. At first, he may agree to attend with her, but his interest begins to wane and he begins pulling away even more from her.

She has changed from the feminine energy she first presented herself as, to a masculine energy, and he already has his own masculine energy, he doesn't want to blend it with hers, he wants a woman, not a man, to date. He feels pressured and pursued and it is usually at this point when he either disappears completely or calls it off verbally when she pressures him to **"talk about where this is going".**

You can hear the death toll ringing the second a woman says **"I want to talk about where this is going"**. Doomed. The average male will exit the conversation as quickly as he can, and exit your life as well when he hears those words.

Why does this happen to so many women?

It's because in our modern culture, **women are more masculine energy than ever before**. They have impressive careers and lifestyles and are accustomed to going after what they want, aggressively, including men. This will work on a *"feminine energy"* male, but not on the masculine energy men you encounter.

So how do you find love if you are a successful career woman prone to masculine energy, *(going after what you want)?*

First and foremost, slow down. When you meet a new male, **don't worry about whether or not HE is going to FALL IN LOVE with you.** Consider whether **YOU could possibly FALL IN LOVE WITH HIM!**

Now, consider your natural energy. If you are interested in a masculine energy male, *(the go-getter type)*, then you have to stay in a feminine energy mode, which is very difficult to do if it is not your natural energy. If you have self-discipline, you can do it, but it won't be easy. This means that until you are in a true relationship setting you do not initiate contact, create dates or otherwise try to steer the connection. You either accept or reject what the male offers. You do not ask for phone numbers or other contact info, but you supply yours when asked.

If you find it impossible to be passive and simply accept or reject, then you must embrace your masculine energy and seek out men who are more feminine energy. This does not mean that they are effeminate in any way, what it means is that they are the more dreamy types, frequently very creative in some way, musically or artistically, and they have no problems allowing a woman to pursue them and steer the relationship. **How will you know?** When you ask him out, he will say yes, when you call him, he will always answer, when you invite him out, he will accept happily, he will have no problems with you pursuing him. **If he balks at any of the above, he's not the right energy for you, move on before you get attached.**

Another key factor is taking your time before becoming physically involved. Women do bond to the men that they have sex with, it's **biological**. Do not have sex with a man until you know that you two are going to enter into a relationship, wait at least six to eight weeks after you start dating to allow this to occur. If you jump right into bed, you are risking bonding to a man that you may not be compatible with. Slow down.

If you are a feminine energy female, or residing in your feminine energy to establish a relationship, stay there! You cannot switch back and forth until the relationship is **ESTABLISHED.** The same goes for the masculine energy women out there. You can't start off doing all the work and then expect him to turn around and start pursuing you. Once you establish your energy stay there until you are truly in a *"couple"*, at that time it is normal for the two of you to vary your energies, but not until then.

If you want to be cherished and put up on a pedestal where he cares about how you feel, you have to be the feminine energy, which means, *NO CALLING, TEXTING, ASKING OUT, STALKING ON THE NET, or other types of a*ssertive behavior, let him come to you, literally.

Until a guy asks you to be exclusive, keep dating others, and do not have sex until he asks you to be exclusive if you are the feminine energy.

If you are the masculine energy, go ahead and be physical with him if you feel so inclined, ask him to be exclusive before you sleep with him though. You will bond the same as your feminine energy sisters, *so be sure that you want to bond to this guy before you do*, but you are the masculine energy, so put it out there.

When you align your energy and know your role, regardless of which energy you find the most suitable for you, your relationships will start to blossom and love and happiness can be found.

Love usually comes naturally when the ingredients between two people are there, when it feels like your relationship is a struggle, it is not going to work and you should move on and not invest any more time and emotion into it! **STOP TRYING TO MAKE EVERY GUY YOU DATE "*THE ONE*"**, when the right guy comes along, things will just pick up their own energy and you won't be anxious about whether or not he is interested, you will know because he will be pursuing you **OR** happily allowing you to pursue him!

The Dating Game

Sex and "The Silly"

A couple of years ago, when I abruptly found myself single and had just become a member of Netflix, I rented the entire series "**Sex and The City**", and watched it faithfully from beginning to end.

I loved the series!!

There were so many **TRUE** points about relationships as adult single women in their thirties and forties that I could relate to, and their portrayal of the ups and downs of relationships, the hook-ups, the bad breakups were all just **TOO** real!

One of the things that I like to do when watching a favorite show is to try to "guesstimate" the astrological influences that drive the well-defined characters. So please just indulge my silliness here!

In my observations of this popular series, I came up with this analysis.

I believe Samantha to be a Water Sign. She was just so sensual and free, she probably was a Sun Sign Scorpio with a Venus in Sagittarius and a Rising Sign of Aquarius. She was sensual to the core, loved her freedom and was a very independent woman capable of intellectualizing any emotional situation. She eventually finds love in an uncommon pairing, with a much younger man, hence my call of Aquarius rising, just a bit "eccentric" in her choices and tastes.

Miranda, now she's fire, strong fire. She doesn't take any nonsense from anyone, is very ambitious, career motivated, very, very independent and she has a hard time accepting the fact that she can be loved and love without benefit of pain. When she finally accepts love into her life, she becomes a self-actualized woman and finds happiness.

Then we have Charlotte. Mother Earth. She starts off as a character who is focused on building and establishing and is actually quite materialistic, and then she evolves into a more open, less judgmental earthly being, finding love in a place that her character, prior to development, would never have looked. Charlotte must have some planets in Water Signs as she does tap into her spirituality as she develops into womanhood.

And Carrie. Oh Carrie. Definitely Air. All Air. Her need to constantly communicate and express herself lends itself to a suspicion of strong Gemini tendencies, along with her ability to carry on an affair with an ex who is married and then HONESTLY tell her current love about it. She seeks the truth in all things, heavy Aquarius influence, and her need to be fair with everyone is definitely Libran in nature. Carrie's quips and quotes and references to the foolish things women do like "Drunk Dialing" could easily become a manual for what "not to do" when entering a relationship. She's so honest about everything that happens to her, and ultimately, she does find her Soul Mate, in, of all people, Big.

I miss that show.

Maybe someday they'll do a follow up with the characters and call it "Sex and the Senile" and enlighten us as to love during our golden years!!!

The Dating Game

"Sex and The Senile" Already Produced?

I was thinking about it, and the sitcom *The Golden Girls*, was pretty much an 80's version of *Sex and the City* for seniors.

I loved that show too!

Think about it.

Carrie = Dorothy = Air

Blanche = Samantha = Water

Rose = Charlotte = Earth

Ma = Miranda (albeit much older and feistier) = Fire

Here I thought it was an original idea for a show, and it's already been done!!!

LOL!!!

Soul Mates

It's not just about love and romance, soul mates are about a lot more than that.

Soul Mate Love Relationships, as previously discussed in my other blogs about the subject, are never easy.

So, if you meet someone and fall in love and enter into a long-term relationship, perhaps even marry, without any major difficulties, does this mean that they are not your Soul Mate? No.

If you meet someone, fall in love, and have MAJOR difficulties, does this mean that they are your Soul Mate? No.

It's a case by case basis.

We do NOT have only ONE Soul Mate. Different Soul Mates teach us (and we teach them) different lessons. Our parents and children or perhaps grandparents usually are Soul Mate relationships.

Maybe our relationship with our significant other is smooth as molasses, that does not mean that they are not our Soul Mate, it means that we have learned the lessons we were to teach each other and are rewarded (Nirvana) by being allowed to be together in happiness.

Maybe our lesson is not the lesson of romantic love, maybe it is how to parent together, or perhaps we produce a terminally ill child together, and although our relationship is solid, we must learn together how to deal with this type of grief.

Frequently, when we have children, they are a Soul Mate from a past life and there is a significant lesson to learn from each other. I know that both of my sons are Soul Mates from past existences, but I also know that their father was not a Soul Mate of mine, it just worked out karmically that we had to cross paths to bring these two particular souls (my sons) to this earth.

When I compared the astrology charts of my children to mine and to my ex-husband I found a very significant number of Soul Mate aspects between their charts and mine, but not between my chart and my ex-husbands, nor between the boys and their father. I couldn't understand it at first. I compared the two boys, and again, major Soul Mate aspects between the brothers, so the lessons to be learned in our little family were between the three souls connected astrologically and oddly did not include their father.

Evidently, whatever karma existed between the boys and their father had already been worked out, or he was a new "Soul Contact" (which I believe), to both of the boys and to myself.

Now, given the situation around our divorce I would have to say that there has been some pretty negative karma built up between my ex and me and between my ex and his two sons by me, but that will work out over time either later in this life or in the next.

Soul Mates are not just romantic partners.

Think about the relationships you had (or didn't have) with your parents. At least one of your birth parents has been connected to you in a previous life. The more intense the relationship with either parent, the more likely it is that there was a Soul Mate connection that brought you to incarnate as their child.

Think of special mentors you met along the way during this life. Again, there was probably some kind of past life connection.

Think of your worst enemies, hopefully you have few, again, a karmic connection most likely exists, and if it didn't before, and you have some intense negative energy between you, you can be sure that you will be working it out at some future date.

Have you ever met someone and for absolutely no logical reason you instantly disliked them?

That is as much of a Soul Mate connection as the ones where we feel an instant rapport with someone.

As to my Soul Mate connections with my sons, they are strikingly different. I am not sure as to how well I am doing with these particular lessons, as single parenting them for the past fifteen years has not been easy.

As a single (divorced) mom, there were times when I must admit that I envied my ex-husband as he had the freedom (I had custody) to totally move on unfettered by the boys. He didn't have to worry about babysitters on a Saturday night or choosing between an interesting date and a little league game, he wasn't around for any of it, he moved out of our state. However, I had to wake up, parent, transport, go to work, come straight home, pick up, parent, feed, clothe, water and parent 24 hours a day seven days a week, alone, for fifteen years.

It put my life on hold in many ways. I don't regret it, but it was difficult to do.

I did my best to make the right choices along the way, but I know that I didn't always choose correctly, and for those things I feel remorseful.

My sons are now 22 and 23, we all three still have our ups and downs, the journey is not over yet, they are still my responsibility, and still, my ex runs free, but perhaps his lack of responsibility toward these children has to do with a lack of a Soul Mate connection from the day they were born……

I don't think I will ever feel that I am not responsible for these boys, (men), even when they are in their fifties and I am in my seventies or eighties. Their pain is my pain, their joy is my joy, their challenges are my challenges. I do not take control, I just offer what guidance and support that I can, ultimately they must face their challenges alone, I just hope that these little Soul Mates of mine have gleaned what they could from what I have strived to teach them so that they can go on to lead happy and productive lives.

Oh, how I ramble, but I hope that as you read this you broaden your own understanding of the Soul Mate connection.

The Dating Game

Gone With the Wind, a Classic Soul Mate Story

"Oh Rhett, Rhett, where will I go? What will I do?" Scarlett cries out to Rhett as he walks away from her into the fog.

Rhett turns, tips his hat and says "Frankly my dear, I don't give a damn" and disappears into the dark foggy night.

Rhett Butler and Scarlett O'Hara, now THAT my dear, although fictional, is a *classic* soul mate story.

The book came out in 1936 and was written by Margaret Mitchell, I read it annually as I love the story so much. In 1936 this book was way ahead of its' time, very racy, and it was "cleaned up" quite a bit for the screenplay.

In the movie, Scarlett only produces a child with Rhett, but in the book, Scarlett has several children with several different men and is not what one would classify as a "good mother", but Rhett loves her despite her callous ways. Survival turns Scarlett into a greedy opportunist (among other things), but yet, Rhett loves her and wants to protect her and cherish her. Scarlett will not accept his love.

The book goes on and tells of all the trials and tribulations and attempts Rhett makes to win Scarlett over, yet she remains untouched, until the very end, when she finally realizes that her "love" for Ashley Wilkes was nothing more than a childish obsession.

Unfortunately for Scarlett, Rhett has exhausted his emotions and the well of love has run dry. Rhett picks up and leaves Scarlett for good (despite the follow up book written by Alexandra Ripley entitled Scarlett, which tries to make it into a happy ending story and takes away from the dramatic ending of the original work).

That is how soul mate stories end if we do not learn the lesson karma has tried to provide us.

According to karmic laws, Rhett and Scarlett would not meet again in Ireland in the same lifetime as presented in the sequel, but would have to wait for a future incarnation and begin all over again amidst equally difficult circumstances as presented in the first novel.

Don't just watch the movie, if you haven't done so already, read this book, there is much more to the story than presented in the film.

The Dating Game

An Experiment in Utilizing Your Feminine Energy

Many of you have been reading and remarking on my blogs concerning "*The Dating Game*" and my writings on masculine and feminine energies.

I am herein going to provide you with an easy to do experiment in utilizing your feminine energy that is fun and yes, kids, you *can* try this at home.

It is very, very simple. My friend Julie and me did this experiment once at Yankee Stadium, and believe you me, it works! (*And it is FUN*).

You can do this experiment alone, or with a friend. (*It is more fun with a friend as you have someone to giggle about the results with*).

For maximum enjoyment, go to a socially crowded place if you can, but it will work just as well in smaller gatherings, you just will have a smaller control group and can't do it as much.

I recommend trying it at a mall, a sporting event, a concert, somewhere where there is a crowd, but any public place will do, even your local grocery store.

When you see a male approaching you, your task is simply to make eye contact *and smile* and hold the subject's gaze for a count of ten while maintaining the smile.......**DO NOT SPEAK!!!** He who speaks first is the masculine energy!

Nine times out of ten, when you hold the subject's gaze and simply smile, the male will greet you. You are nearly guaranteed to receive a smile in return at a rate of 99.99%! When Julie and I conducted this experiment we got return smiles in each and every case and in 99 out of 100 trials, we got a greeting, a hello, and each of us was approached to converse with ten different times.

All we did was smile...and maintain eye contact for a count of ten.

It's amazing and it is good practice for drawing a male to you when you see one that you are actually interested in.

Try it! It works!

The Dating Game

Relationships from All Angles

(The Geometry of Relationships)

Being an Aquarian, and prone to be analytical and logical about all things, inclusive of relationships, I have begun thinking of relationships in relation to Mathematics and in particular, Geometry.

Geometry is a very intricate subject, used by many of the sciences as the ground work for such things as physics, engineering and more. Let's apply Geometry to the World of Relationships.

First and foremost, the most obvious Geometric Shape that all are aware of is the Triangle, or, more specifically, ***"The Love Triangle"***.

A "***Love Triangle***" is generally defined by the presence of three entities who are involved emotionally, usually with two of the entities forming the base of the triangle, and one of the entities, (the one involved with both entities at the base), forming the vertex. Frequently it is an equilateral triangle, where the person in the position of the vertex is trying to juggle both "angles" to the persons at the base in a seemingly balanced way.

The Love Triangle can be the Geometry of an affair outside of a marriage, or a relationship outside of what is believed to be the **"Primary Relationship"** of the Vertex Person. The **"Primary Relationship"** is usually the relationship that the Vertex Person keeps very public and in the open, the Base Person in the Primary Relationship is usually unaware of the congruent relationship with the Secondary Relationship and is moving forward in good faith that their relationship with the Vertex Person is exclusive.

The Secondary Relationship Base Person is usually aware of the Primary Relationship Base Person but for a myriad of reasons, although aware that their relationship is not exclusive with the Vertex Person, they continue to invest time, energy and love and emotion into supporting the Base of the Triangle.

The Dating Game

The Geometry of the Love Triangle is not positive for anyone involved, ultimately one of the entities in the Geometry of this Triangle will be hurt, if not all.

Love Triangles can be **"Acute Triangles"** that tend to draw the Vertex Person to one side, usually away from the Primary Relationship, but the angle to the Primary Base Person is not broken. They can be in the form of an "Equilateral Triangle", whereby the Vertex Person is trying to maintain a balanced angle to both persons at the base. Then there is the "Obtuse Triangle", where neither person at the Base Positions is aware of their congruent opposite. Many forms of Triangular Relationships exist, and they are, to say the least, a difficult and unbalanced Relationship Geometry.

Let's move on to a different Relationship Geometric, the **"Square"**. The Square is the most popular and sought after Relationship Geometric, although, it can be a bit bland or boring for the more adventurous among us.

The "*Relationship Square*" is very traditional in aspect. It is the same length on all sides. It can represent the stable couple moving through life, firmly and balanced, the nuclear family with the million dollar family, (a son and daughter), or the couples who settle for the shape of things as they have no desire to change the shape of their future, either because they are comfortable or because they lack ambition.

Square Relationships don't allow too many factors into the area of their relationship. They don't seek adventure, they are fairly self-contained. Socialization is most likely limited to close friends and family and values are usually traditional. Adventure and passion are not part of the Geometry of the Square, but stability and security are.

Many people choose to stay within their Square for fear of change. Squares are at high risk for becoming Triangles at some point in time, as angles are ever changing and one side of the Square may change over time, mutilating the shape of the Square into the Triangle.

The Dating Game

Squares are uncomplicated Relationships. The boundaries are well-defined and as long as none of the sides of the Square change in shape, the Square stays intact.

The **"Relationship Rectangle"** is similar to the Relationship Square in many ways, however, the sides of the Rectangle are not all the same length, although the dynamics are similar, there is more room for the parties within the Rectangle to stretch and grow and the area encompassed is a little broader or wider.

Rectangles are stable Relationships that allow more input from outside sources, yet still very secure for the parties involved.

The **"Relationship Parallelogram"** is a very interesting one. It usually pertains to entities that are living "Parallel Lives" and frequently, they are the unmanifested Soul Mate relationships of this lifetime.

We may find many synchronistic characteristics in the Relationship Parallelogram, never truly crossing paths, but never truly being disconnected. Sometimes we are together, sometimes apart, but always in sync with each other.

My favorite Relationship Geometric is the **"Relationship Circle"** and the simplest way to explain it is to liken it to coming **Full Circle**. We are round, we can roll like a wheel with change, we've faced challenges and obstacles and still our shape is intact. Perhaps we started off as a Square and the challenges time brings as we moved along forced us to lose our rough edges so that we could be mobile and roll, or perhaps we started off as a Triangle or went from Square to Triangle to Circle, it makes no difference.

The Circle can grow, but it never loses its' shape. It can expand to increase its' area, but it does not lose its shape, it can shrink to close in to protect itself, but it never loses its shape.

To me, the Relationship Circle is the best and most dynamic Relationship Geometric, and I find it to be the happiest in the long run.

You can always expand or contract your circle as you adjust, and the Circle is the easiest to transport through life's transitions, it can actually carry you, instead of you carrying it.

So, that is my view on **The Geometry of Relationships.**

The Dating Game

Chapter Two

Transitioning Into/Out of Relationships

The Dating Game

The Dating Game

I Want It All, And I Want It Now!

Great Song by Queen! One of my favorite bands, by the way.

I certainly understand the sentiment behind the song, and it is perfectly fine to want it all and want it now, but, my dearest, sometimes *Patience truly is a Virtue*.

I have had many, many clients over the years, with situations at varying degrees of difficulty, and we have worked through them successfully together. There were times when a learning curve may have slowed or delayed progress, but we got through the toughest times with a high degree of success.

The learning curve seems to always come with my clients when it comes to communication. Many do not and will not simply wait out a situation to allow it to change. As discussed in my multiple blogs on_ *Masculine and Feminine Energy*, it seems that a large percentage of female clients cannot self-discipline themselves to the feminine *(passive)* energy when it comes to communication.

Despite our work together, they decide not to follow the advice of the cards, and the natural balance between *Masculine and Feminine Energy*, and they initiate contact with the object of their desires first *(masculine energy)*. All is not lost, however, any progress that was made during their self-imposed silence has now been erased and has lost any and all effectiveness in allowing the male to feel their absence and grow uncomfortable. Now the male does not have a motivating factor *(discomfort)* to produce any change in his behavior.

By initiating contact the female has now condoned whatever his unacceptable behavior was and basically trained him that it is okay to treat her like this *(inattentively)*.

So although the woman now has the immediate gratification of having communication and contact with the object of her desires, she has now, inadvertently, taken a few steps backwards into establishing her feminine energy and has most likely delayed any significant change in the males' behavior.

Why? Because now, you have reassured the male in question that yes, indeed, you are still actively interested in him. **So why change his behavior?** If he doesn't feel like calling you for another week or two, you don't mind, you just trained him that you will reach out to him if he doesn't reach out to you, you will do all the *"work"*, and if he feels like being accessible to you he will, if he doesn't, he won't. You have taught him that your feelings don't matter, you don't warrant his attention because on the peripheral, you will still be there. He has absolutely no fear *(motivation)* that your attention will wander, after all, it's been two weeks since he called you and here you are ringing him up telling him that you miss him!! He knows he has you, has no fear that you will go away, so why would he change?

Now, you've made the contact, expressed your feelings, he was glad to hear from you, the phone call has ended, and guess what? **He goes silent again.**

You have, in effect, told him, in no uncertain terms that he can go about his busy life and when he has the time or the need for your companionship, you'll still be over here in _**limbo**_ waiting...no worries for him.

The need for immediate emotional gratification is the same need that throws the timing of most relationships off when you succumb to it.

What is immediate emotional gratification?

It is infantile in nature. Immediate gratification is the *"immediate"* fulfilling of a need, as in when an infant cries because they are hungry and the mother rushes to feed the child. This is good, this is responsible motherhood and necessary to build a sense of security within any newborn child.

We are not babies, sorry to say. We are grown men and women and we should be able to discipline ourselves to reap the benefits of delayed gratification.

What is delayed gratification?

Delayed gratification is being able to wait to have your needs fulfilled at a more permanent and stable level. For example, the student who wants to become an attorney and works through four years of college and then attends law school and delays the *"gratification"* of going out and working full time in order to buy the nice car they have their eye on. The goal is not to have a nice car at the age of 22, but to have a good career and an even nicer car *(and overall lifestyle)* at the age of 25 or 26 or so. Delayed gratification is a sign of mature and responsible adulthood.

How do these two differing types of gratification work into the ***Geometry of Relationships***?

Ok, immediate gratification leads you to make those phone calls to the object of your desire and having that immediate relief that the contact may bring. It feels good, your needs are satisfied, your thirst for his voice is quenched, for now. As discussed above, you are now most likely going to go back into the waiting mode and either reach for immediate gratification again or suffer it out and wait for the delayed gratification.

With the delayed gratification approach you will suffer now, in the immediate, you will be uncomfortable, you will be wondering why he doesn't reach out, but you do not reach out to him, you wait it out. As discussed in multiple other blogs found under my category "***Brigid Bishop, Relationship Coach***", you busy yourself with other matters, other dates, and you do not reach out at all. It is not easy and it takes self-discipline, but it can be done.

Your absence and the absence of your energy will draw him out if he truly does care, and if he does not, if it is over, your life will not be empty while you wait it out, you will have other people to socialize with and other males to investigate relationship opportunities with in the interim. It is possible that you will even find a male who is a better match for you than the original object of your affections.

If you can abstain and wait for the delayed gratification, the male in question will be reaching out to you because you have allowed him the time to miss you, to realize that he misses you. Your prolonged absence will also have him change his behavior toward you as he will be well aware that you will not be sitting on a shelf waiting for him to rescue you from ***limbo***.

Which would you prefer?

The instant rush of the immediate gratification ***(satisfying an infantile need)*** and the continuing ***Relationship Limbo*** or the short-term ***(it could be months, but short-term in the big picture)*** discomfort and the delayed, and long lasting gratification that effects change in your relationship dynamic? ***(Satisfaction at a mature adult level).***

The choice is up to you, but in my extensive experience in working with clients in these types of situations, the latter is preferable as it is permanent change for the better and not just fleeting happiness.

The Dating Game

Independence, Codependence and Interdependence

Where are you at with your relationship style?

Independence?

In "Deep End"-ness

Co "Deep End"-ness

Inter "Deep End"-ness

Picture the realm of relationships as a big swimming pool. You are in the deep end of the pool.

If you are in *"independent"* mode, you are swimming around all by yourself, doing fine, getting out and diving in off the high dive, unaffected by the other swimmers around you. You are an individual and you are not connecting with others at this time, you are focused on yourself and yourself alone. You may take an occasional date with another swimmer, but you prefer to swim alone most of the time.

If you are in *"codependent"* mode, well, you won't go in the water alone. Someone must always be with you. A lifeguard must always be on duty. When you dive in you immediately swim over to another swimmer and begin to cling on to them, they frequently push you away. You may feel like you are drowning and no one is helping you. The more you try to cling to another swimmer, the more you are pushed away. You thrash around, swallow water and end up hanging on to the side of the pool coughing and crying. It's not much fun in the pool for you, but you keep trying.

If you are in *"interdependent"* mode, you have a great time at the relationship pool. You have one special partner that you swim with on a regular basis. You may synchronize your swim into a beautiful dance in the waters of relationship, when you go to the diving board to try a new move, your partner is there in the water below waiting and watching to be sure you are safe, spotting you while you dive, and you do the same for them. When your swim time is over, you are both comfortable going your separate ways as you know that you will meet back at the pool again soon for another dip, and you feel secure about the other person.

I am a firm believer in interdependence. Independence is fine, it is healthy, but in relationships we have to know how to let people in. Independence can become lonely if we refuse to join in the fun going on in the relationship pool. There are times when we want to be alone, perhaps we are healing over a bad breakup or just not ready because we have other priorities right now, raising children or career, etc., but don't swim alone for so long that you forget how to connect.

Codependence is a horrible, anxiety-ridden state to exist in. We feel like we are nothing unless we can define ourselves by our relationships, behaviors while in codependent mode can escalate to cyber stalking, and worse, physical stalking. We want others in our lives so bad that we drive them away because we don't have the self-discipline to let our relationships develop naturally. We tend to go through relationships faster and in higher numbers than most. They all seem to start off promising enough, but within a month or two we are back on the side of the pool crying and coughing. If you are in codependent mode, it may be wise for you to try the independent mode for several months to readjust your relationship goggles and your approach to relationships in general. Once we have mastered independence, we have a much higher success rate at moving on to interdependence.

Ah, interdependence, it is the way all healthy relationships should operate. You and your loved one are secure in knowing that you are there for each other, you are capable of being together, happily, and also of pursuing other interests and friendships without fear or insecurity. There is no need to check up on each other or doubt anything because you have established trust, respect and love. To gain interdependence you and your partner must spend the necessary time in the relationship pool, getting to know each other and enjoying each other, but you must also learn to respect each other's boundaries and to give each other space.

What is your style of swimming in the relationship pool?

The Newly – "Bed" Game

No, not another post about my recent marriage, but a thoughtful post about client concerns once they have physically consummated their latest relationship...

Ok, you've taken the plunge. You made love to your newest flame because, let's face it, things got hot and you were swept up in the moment.

You've been attracted to him for some time, and you believe that making love to him is going to bond him to you and make him want you more.

Sometimes that is true, and it is very self-evident because he goes into hot pursuit of you, and he wants more of your time, and more of your physical love and you have nothing to worry about, you are happy and your relationship is growing in its' physical connection, or is it?

How can you tell if this is just a *"physical thing"* or if you are on your way to a solid relationship?

Sex is an important part of the bond that grows between a man and a woman, and a strong sexual bond can actually create a firm foundation for emotional gratification, it's very hard for a man to walk away from great sex, the thing is, is that all it is?

Ways to tell if your newly-bed game is a healthy sexual interchange or just a roll in the hay:

He calls you promptly and frequently to talk, to set up a date (*a real date, a social event, not coming over to your house when your kids are asleep to get more sex*). He lingers after the sex act is completed, he doesn't jump up and say "I have an early meeting tomorrow, have to run, call you soon", when he does leave he kisses you and tells you **_WHEN_** he is going to call.

The Dating Game

The time you spend together is spent doing a variety of things, not just bumping uglies. For example, on a Friday night you catch a movie, go for a drink or two, talk and then when he takes you home it's up to you whether or not you invite him into your home and/or your heart. It's not a good sign if he shows up at your house on a Friday night after 11 and sweeps you off to the bedroom after you've been sitting by the phone all week waiting for him to call you.

All romantic relationships need physical and sexual chemistry to progress. The trick is all in the timing. How soon should you allow him to enjoy physical intimacy with you?

There is no pat answer. We are all different in our value systems, our physical desires, etc., the main thing I want you to consider is how _**YOU**_ feel about laying yourself open to connecting in this manner, as a woman. The issue is all about female biology. Females tend to bond emotionally to a male they mate with due to the pheromones in her system. This is nature's cruel trick on our species. This "bonding" biology is absent in the male biology as they are genetically programmed to impregnate as many fertile females as they can to ensure the survival of the species. Although humans have evolved into thinking entities, these natural biological facts still hold true in our modern culture. For a male to "bond" emotionally, it takes much more than a sexual act, (*sometimes I think it is purely an "act of God" when they do*), it takes a conscious decision on their part that you are their woman of choice.

I would recommend that you not allow yourself to enjoy the physical consummation of your relationship with the new guy too soon, definitely not on the first or second date. The longer you can wait, the more the heated anticipation builds between you, and the more intense your ultimate physical gratification will be for both of you. If it is, indeed, very intense the first time, you can expect that the male in question will want more of the same.

So, we are back to _**delayed gratification vs. immediate gratification**_.

I would suggest that as a female you wait at least long enough to be certain that the male has a sincere interest in you. That he is willing to wait until you are comfortable being sexually intimate, and that he is willing to court you and treat you with respect and thoughtfulness while you are learning what kind of partner he is.

If you have spent a few weeks with missed phone calls, poorly planned dates and neglectful behavior, I would say, don't bond to him, don't make love to him, having sex is not going to improve your situation, it is only going to make you chemically bond to him and intensify your anxiety when he behaves poorly. However, if he is attentive, treats you well, if he makes time for you and appreciates you and you are feeling that you are being romanced, (consistently), well, then perhaps it is time to give him a little loving!

The most significant recommendation I can give to you before you newly-bed a new man, is that he should be making you feel that he is consistent in his attentions. He should be sincere in his courtship of you, in so much as he is trying to show you what a good guy he is, spend time with you, take you out, and make you feel appreciated.

The Dating Game

REAL MEN DON'T CALL PSYCHICS!

(What Women Want)

Oh, so **NOT TRUE!!** Although most of my blogging has been aimed at my female audience, this is "**One for the Boys**".

Yes, my client base is 75% female, but 10% of my clients are heterosexual males. (The remaining 15% are gay and lesbian).

The reason for this is women, by nature, tend to reach out and express emotions, while men, by nature try to be self-sufficient and are more hesitant to reach out for advice, especially psychic advice, as it is so hard for them to quantify it.

Regardless, **REAL MEN DO CALL PSYCHICS!** (And ladies, they frequently have the same issues we do, but they come at them from an entirely different perspective).

I love men. I have been a flirt all of my life, knowingly and unknowingly, and I have never had a shortage of men in my life. I am currently married for the second time in my life, and I would like to tell my male customers some secrets about "**What Women Want**".

Oh, the things most women want...

Women like communication. When you meet a female of the species and you interact with her, and have a mutually pleasant encounter, and you have asked her for her number.....she actually does expect you to call! Of course, you don't want to appear over anxious, so you may not call her the very next day, but by the second day after an encounter like this, the average female is jumping up to read the caller ID every time her phone rings. So, take a hint. If you meet a woman you are interested in and she gives you her number, please contact her relatively soon, if you truly are interested. If you are not interested, please don't ask her for her number in the first place. Don't play games with her, respect her feelings.

*Women like "**plans**"*. Don't wait until Friday afternoon after work to call her for the weekend. If you'd like to see a woman on the weekend, give her a call by Wednesday, Thursday at the absolute latest. This way she knows you put some thought into seeing her and she doesn't feel like it was a "what the hell, I'm not doing anything else tonight, let me ring her up." Women like plans and they may hold off making plans with friends waiting for you to call. Respect her time and realize that, unknowingly, you may be holding her back socially. This way, if you call her on a Wednesday and you know you are going on a fishing trip for the weekend, she is aware and can move forward with her own plans. Yes, I know, you didn't make plans, but women hold a "spot" open "just in case" very frequently. Release her from her bonds of "maybe he'll call".

Women **DO NOT** like to be **STALKED**. If she has been avoiding you and your phone calls let it go. Some women are not good at being direct about being disinterested. If it's too difficult to get her on the phone or she doesn't return your messages, please move on.

Women, again, like plans. Please do not call her up and ask to see her on the weekend and then say "***what do you want to do***", this puts her in a difficult position as there are literally a million different things "***to do***". When you are ready to call her and ask her out, have an idea or two about what to do. Ask her if she'd like to go to dinner or if she'd like to see the newest movie that's out, something to that effect, don't put the pressure on her to choose. Women like plans!!!

Women like attention. If you have been seeing her for awhile and you really do care for her and want to continue seeing her, flowers are always appropriate. Women love to receive flowers. Especially at work where other women can see that someone does care about them!

Women like to feel cared about. When you two are talking, ask her how she feels about the different subjects you discuss. Ask her how she feels about how things are going....if asked, she will tell you.

Women like progress. Make mention, as your relationship progresses, of what you think about how things are moving along. Tell her that you think things are going well. Tell her that you think you have a future.

Women like honesty. Please don't lie to women. It is very upsetting to them. Even the little white lies hit women like darts in the eyeball, so try to be as honest as you can with them. It is better to suffer a little discomfort by answering a question you are uncomfortable with honestly than to tell a lie, get caught, and have the woman you think you may be falling in love with go ballistic on you and hearing about it for the next ten years.

Women like commitment. If you care for her and you believe that you love her, tell her. Think out loud about the future with her, but remember, women like honesty, so don't do it if you don't mean it. If you are not into commitment then you should be playing the field and not dating one woman exclusively, and you should be honest about it.

Women like security. If circumstances exist that make it difficult to see each other as much as you would like, such as travel for business, etc., make an extra effort to stay in communication, make plans, send flowers, etc., it will ease her insecurities and build a happy foundation.

Women like romance. Flowers, candy, opening her car door for her, getting the door as you enter and exit buildings, dancing, candlelight, telling her a song reminds you of her, telling her sweet things and being creative with the time you spend together, these things make her feel warm and loving toward you.

Women like to feel connected. If you are dating and you want to continue to do so, give her something personal of yours to keep, like a favorite t-shirt or sweatshirt that has some symbolic meaning to her. She will wear it, sleep in it, tell her friends about it and be very happy about it. Women like to feel connected to you.

Just a glimpse, very straightforward, of what the majority of women of all ages do like and hope for in a relationship, even in our modern times.

Stop, Drop and Roll!

Remember learning this when you were a child?

It tells you how to put out a fire.

The next time that you are trying to start up a new relationship and you are tempted to *"Stop, Drop and Roll"* for the new man in your life, think more carefully about whether the time is right to be intimate.

There is no magic number for the number of dates, weeks, or months to begin to be intimate with the man in question. There are many mitigating factors.

First of all, what type of a relationship are you hoping for this to develop into?

If you are just casually dating and have no desire for this to blossom into a serious relationship and would like to be physically gratified, then by all means, *"Stop, Drop and Roll"* for him.

However, if you are hoping that this relationship will develop into something a bit deeper, try using these keywords to determine if it is the right time to allow yourself to bond physically and psychologically with this man.

Stop. How attentive is he? Is he consistent with calling when he says he will, seeing you on a regular basis, keeping dates and making you feel wanted?

Drop. Has he dropped any other women he is dating or is he still playing the field?

Roll. Do you have fun together? Roll with laughter? Can you picture yourself rolling forward with him into the future as he is now, or do you imagine changing him as you progress?

Why do I say this? *Is it because my moral barometer is set on 1950?* No, not at all. Although your individual moral values will be your primary guide as to when the time is right for you, there are actually biological reasons why should consider delaying sexual gratification with a new partner.

The female brain will produce **dopamine** and **oxytocin** during sexual activity, these two hormones will cause the female to bond to the male in question due to nature's cruel programming trick to ensure procreation of the species. We may be living in a new millennium, but our brains still function at a prehistoric level when it comes to survival of the species.

So, if you proceed with physical intimacy prior to going through the "*Stop, Drop and Roll*" process you may find yourself physiologically binding to a man who will not *Stop* being inattentive, has not *Dropped* other women, and who wants to *Roll* in the hay with you and any other women he may be dating.

Is this what you want? Chemicals being released into your body causing you to bond to him before he is ready, willing and able to bond to you? You will be finding that even the scent of this man may set off the chemical release, causing a physiological reaction that creates a bond with a partner that is not right for you.

So, when is the right time to become physically intimate?

When he *STOPS* and uses his time to pursue you.

When he **DROPS** other women and the pursuit of other women.

When he **ROLLS** forward with you exclusively.

Stop, Drop and Roll will put out any flash fires and allow you to fan the flames of true love.

Set yourself up for successful relationships, **Stop, Drop and Roll!**

The Dating Game

How Do YOU Like Your Eggs?

A good question that all women should ask themselves.

It never ceases to amaze me how little nuances in movies and books can actually awaken one to an important life lesson. It happens to me all the time. Are you absorbing the "Life Lessons" that mass media is trying to communicate to you?

Do you actually remember the scene from the movie *"Runaway Bride"* starring Julia Roberts and Richard Gere?

He pressed her to figure out what her preference was for the style of eggs she enjoyed eating. It seems that Julia's character made whatever her current love interests' favorites were her own favorites, rather than allowing her own tastes to develop.

Every time Julia's character fell in love, she lost herself in the shadow of the male that she was interested in, mimicking his tastes and interests rather than developing and sharing her own.

I call these types of women "Shadow Women".

I know quite a few.

Here is an example.

I have a good friend, let's call her Rachel.

Rachel is a very pretty and vivacious thirty-one year old, divorced, mother of three.

Rachel is a serial monogamist, quite adept at *making love out of nothing at all*.

The Dating Game

She chooses her target, (man), and quite invisibly stalks him and becomes a part of his world (and his significant other), without the male really taking notice. She is a Cancer Woman with the Moon in Scorpio, very smooth operator who appears quite innocent.

Anyway, here is how she "works it".

First, she finds out what his interests are, the things that he is passionate about. Then she immerses herself in them to the point of obsession. With the first gentleman I watched her snare this way, it was motorcycles and rock'n'roll. Rachel learned to ride a motorcycle, got certified as a motorcycle mechanic, learned the guitar, started singing regularly in public via Karaoke, and eventually helped form a band that she convinced her target, who happened to be a drummer, to join. All she walked, talked, lived and breathed during this five year long "stalk", er, uh, relationship, was motorcycles, mechanics, the "band" (which never played a gig, but practiced quite a lot), and such.

The surprising thing was, she was still married to her first husband when all of this began. It was about a one-year period from the beginning of her infatuation until the dissipation of the marriage, which was not very pleasant for any involved.

Sad part is, target guy didn't know that he was the reason behind all this and still thought of himself as Rachel's "friend", although he did enjoy a benefit during that first year that did produce her third child and his first.

So stage one is getting into HIS world and abandoning your own, dissatisfactory one.

Second, she "tracks" him, finds out his schedule and movements during an average week, and then suddenly his schedule is mysteriously coinciding with HER schedule. What a coincidence!

Third, with barely a ripple on the surface, and perhaps a good two years or so into the "hunt", he somehow finds himself in relationship mode with her. Usually due to some crisis she experiences that leaves her needing a place to live, with her kids, and abracadabra! They're living together!

Now she has what she thought she wanted. This is usually around year three. Now the rapid decline as she finds she likes her eggs scrambled and not boiled sets in and she becomes malcontent with the relationship.

Usually this is the point where the man is really realizing that he is "into" her and wants to continue or deepen the commitment.

This is the point where Rachel finds a new target!

She's living with motorcycle dude and she meets golf dude!

Wow!

He's a much better deal!

While living with motorcycle dude she begins swinging her relationship trapeze over toward golf dude.

Suddenly a sport that she found boring and pretentious for twenty-five years or so is fascinating!

She watched all the tournaments on TV, memorized statements made by sports commentators on winners and losers, gets a job at a local golf course as a waitress in the clubhouse, (of course it's where HE golfs), bought golf clubs she COULD NOT afford, and started laying the groundwork for breaking up with motorcycle dude.

So, she moved out of the house motorcycle dude bought to build a life with her and moved into an apartment above the local bar that golf dude tended at part time and hung out at all the time.

Here it is, three years later, and over the past six months she moved in with golf dude (her landlord threw her out with no notice….hmmm…..not the first time), and just recently, they rented a house "together" with her three children in tow.

Now she no longer rides or tinkers with motorcycles or dresses in leather and jeans.

Now she has that "preppy" look and golfs with golf dude in tournaments she can't afford, but finds a way to pay for, and she has sold her guitar and her motorcycle to pay for a set of custom golf clubs. This is a woman with little resources, who cannot afford this type of luxury, yet, in order to conduct her shadow relationship, she sacrifices her children's needs in lieu of her codependent shadowing.

I can predict exactly what will happen. Golf dude will become comfortable and stable and long for a deeper commitment. Perhaps even the "m" word. Shadow friend will start seeing that she is bored with golf and preppiness and will develop an interest in a future "target" and start her relationship trapeze up while still living with golf dude, perhaps this time it will be a rodeo cowboy or a Nascar driver or an astronaut!!

Watch her interests change!

So, what kind of eggs do you prefer?

Do you know?

Do you develop your own interests or do you immerse yourself in the interests of those whom you would like to have a relationship with?

There is nothing wrong with someone you are interested in introducing you to a different lifestyle, or getting you to try something new. That's wonderful! However, don't lose yourself in the process!

Think of it this way.

The Dating Game

If you were NOT involved with THIS PERSON, would you still have an interest in this activity or event? If so, great! If not, you're doing it to "fit in" to the other person's life and you would be better served, (and more interesting to OTHER PEOPLE) to pursue your own interests and develop yourself into the self-actualized woman you were meant to be.

How much smoother relationships run when they are not forced, but come about naturally, based on truly common interests and value systems!

How much more interesting you will be to other people, including even that cute guy you are currently trapezing toward, when you have knowledge and activities of your own to talk about and share and introduce him to!

Shared interests are great, don't get me wrong, but don't just become the shadow of your partner, keep your individuality as well!

By the way, my friend Rachel, she is also of the type who lets all of her other relationships fall by the wayside while in hot pursuit and development of a new shadow. Guess what? When the crisis point comes when she wants to cut her shadow feet off of the guy she has most recently attached herself to, she has a very difficult time coping because many of her friends feel abandoned by her obsession with the new guy and are hesitant to be supportive of her.

I always welcome her back in, however, I will write another blog about the importance of maintaining your friendships while in relationship mode. Soon.

Sunny-Side UP!

The Dating Game

If You Can't Be With The One You Love, Love the One You're With

(The Proper "Usage" of the Transitional Man)

Okay girls, we've all had them. These are the guys that we spend time with in between our major love relationships. They serve as a bridge from breaking up to making up, or new love.

Frequently they are the guys that we consider to be *"friends"*, but who have a deeper interest in us. Oh, come on, don't lie or try to fool yourself. Your lunchtime buddy at work who always wants you to meet up with him for a drinkie poo after work and listens to all your cares and concerns about your romantic misadventures is frequently one of these *"friends"* and may well be lending an ear to get closer to some of **YOUR** body parts.

Or he's the guy you met on the internet dating service that looks great on paper, (or online), but just doesn't have that *"chemistry"* we need.

Sometimes he's the guy that chases and pursues us when our egos are bruised and eventually we just give in because hell, it feels good to be appreciated.

But just the same, a key ingredient to the potion that causes us to *"fall in love"* is missing.

We're out there.

We're accepting that our relationship with our beloved is over and we are moving on.

Remember, the term *"Transitional Man"* applies to that gentleman whom we are dating, casually, but not likely to form a permanent relationship with because although he may be a great guy, he's just not in possession of the qualities that we need.

The Dating Game

A mistake women frequently make while utilizing the growth period of **"*transition between relationships*"** is to try to force a round peg into a square hole and make a **"*Transitional Man*"** into the **"*Significant Other*"**.

Oh, I've done it myself.

After my divorce back in 1992 I dated, with full intent of only allowing the guy to be Mr. Transition a fellow that **_I KNEW_** was all wrong for me. He was the extreme opposite of my ex-husband, and very irresponsible in his lifestyle, he was also the extreme opposite of me, but, unfortunately, I just let myself become **"*comfortable*"** with him as I was too lazy to move on and I ended up wasting five years in a relationship that should have expired after about six months.

Why did I allow this to happen?

Well, I was a newly divorced single mother with two preschoolers, almost impossible to get out and meet new people as I was struggling to survive, let alone afford a babysitter on any kind of regular basis. This was pre-internet dating (**_boy, I sure would've shopped around more had that been available_**), and I kind of just **"settled"** for keeping company with him.

It was easy.

He would come to my house when I couldn't come out.

He would eat my food.

He would watch my TV.

He would use anything I had around the house for his own comfort and convenience.

What he **_DIDN'T_** do was get a job.

He **DIDN'T** help me with the kids.

He **DIDN'T** grow up and behave responsibly.

I noticed, but I didn't care because it staved off loneliness, and as I said, it was easy.

While he lay around at his mother's house during the day collecting workmen's compensation for an injury that should have been a day or two off (**he still doesn't work by the way**), I was out building my career as an Operations Manager at a Printing Corporation **AND** paying top dollar for daycare and babysitting.

When I came home from work, he would somehow manage to show up at my house right around the time dinner was being served and mooch a free meal.

He was kind to my kids, but more like a big, Baby Huey than a father figure.

I never let him sleep over because of my children, so he was gone by eleven at night.

Was he committed? Well, it depends on your definition. Exclusive physically to me, yes, committed, **NO!!!**

So anyway, one day, while I was purchasing my home in 1996 (*by myself, for me and my kids*), I realized that I had got caught up and trapped in transition! I had never moved forward successfully into a new and healthy relationship with a new partner, I had just stayed "in transition" for five years. Had I been in a truly committed relationship I wouldn't be buying a home by myself, I would've been buying it with a life partner.

I ended it that week.

The Dating Game

The way I should have handled that situation was that I should have, after a six month period, realized that I was not in love with this guy, I was just comfortable with his company and living by the Crosby, Stills, Nash and Young Anthem of "*If you can't be with the one you love, love the one you're with*".

I never truly loved that guy.

I liked him.

I was not physically, chemically or sexually attracted to him, but exposing myself to his company over time allowed him to "grow on me", (*like a fungus*), so that I did bond to him, but I never loved him.

He did not have the same type of life goals as me, he did not have any ambition, and he did not match well with me in any area except that of enjoying spending leisure time together (*hell, all __he had__ was leisure time*).

So the lesson here is, while you are in between relationships, or just recently coming out of a relationship, please be sure to use your time with a "*Transitional Man*" wisely. Learn to **RECOGNIZE** that the guy's purpose in your life may not be to become your life partner, but just to keep you company for a little while until you **DO** find your next **Significant Other**.

When that little sick feeling inside you comes up when you are wondering if the guy is right for you, listen to it, don't ignore it, and don't just let things ride because they are comfortable and familiar, step back and choose wisely. Don't be afraid to end it with your "*Transitional Man*". Every man you date **IS NOT** a potential life mate, they are few in number and they will not evoke that sick "should I keep seeing this guy even though he hasn't had a job in six months" feeling.

In my case, my irresponsible transitional man made me feel youthful again at the age of twenty-nine after my marriage to my ex-husband had made me feel like I was a century old, and I got charmed by his sheer lack of responsibility to the world, even though I was an extremely responsible woman. What I didn't realize was that he had no responsibility to me, either, and I needed someone who would choose to be responsible to me as well. I did find him, but hell, *I kissed a lot of frogs that were passing through*.

Is your current guy just a *"Transitional Man"* or is he *"The Real Thing"*?

Expect More, Pay Less

No, this isn't a *"Target"* commercial, I'm just borrowing their catch phrase for this little blog.

I took a break one night at 10 p.m. to watch **Law and Order SVU**, one of my favorite shows, (actually an addiction of mine), and this over-used phrase came up on a **Target Commercial** and it made me think of some of my clients, and the discomfort they are going through.

Right now (and on any given day during any given year), I have no less than three dozen clients who are going through difficulties in relationships, and are paying their "relationship dues".

I want them to concentrate on this phrase.

"Expect More, Pay Less".

Now, each of you who is a client of mine and reading this may think that I am writing this directly for you, however, I am not writing this for any one individual, I am writing it to you as a conglomerate. It may help you to know that you are not alone, this message is for many of you to consider.

Okay, back to the phrase.

"Expect More, Pay Less".

Right now you may be in any one of these phases; waiting for him to call, waiting for him to ask you out, waiting for him to come back, etc., but you are not happy. You are expecting very little. A phone call or an email just to get validation that he knows you are still in existence.

For this emotional state you are paying an extremely high toll. You may be one, or any combination of the following; anxious, depressed, worried, sad, hopeful, nervous, lonely, angry, etc.

This price is too high.

My message to you, my dear friends, is….

EXPECT MORE, PAY LESS!!!

Don't pour your self-esteem down the drain by checking your email hourly to see if there is some innocuous message from him!

Don't cruise "myspace" or "facebook" to see who his newest friends are!!

Don't cruise "match" to see if his listing is active!!!

Don't run to the phone to check the caller ID each time it rings!!!

Don't check for a dial tone!!!

Don't panic if you leave the house to run to the store and forget your cell phone!!!!

EXPECT that he will call, but don't have your life revolving around it.

EXPECT that he will ask you out, but date others until he does!

EXPECT that he will treat you with care, concern and respect for your feelings, and if he doesn't, *RUN*, don't walk away.

Expect that he will realize what a wonderful human being that you are and that you are totally lovable and that you deserve to be treated well, and he will! If he does not, he's not worth the emotional price.

When you start *EXPECTING* to be treated correctly, you will stop *PAYING SO MUCH* emotionally.

The Dating Game

Is a three sentence email or a forwarded joke to a mass mailing list worth wasting the time running to your computer?

Is a phone call that is slow in coming worth wasting four nights out of the week anxiously sitting by your phone, waiting, when you could be out doing something you enjoy?

NO!

EXPECT MORE, PAY LESS!!!!

Please give these four little words some serious consideration.

Why Men Are Like Buses!

I have mentioned this quote from a wise woman in one of my other blogs, but I think it worthy of expounding on the analogy.

It's funny that while I was married to my first husband I did not fully appreciate the wisdom of my first mother-in-law, alas, we live and we learn.

When I was divorcing her son after our eight year long marriage I was having coffee with her while she was paying a visit to see my two sons, her beloved grandchildren, and we were speaking about the difficulties encountered in relationships. It may well have been one of the best conversations we ever had over the years that we were family.

Anyway, I was twenty-nine years old at the time, and she actually did support my decision to divorce her son.

Her sage advice was this, and I quote, "***Brigid, men are like buses, you stand on the corner long enough and another one comes along***". At the time, I burst out laughing because I couldn't believe that she was actually saying this to me! Her future ***EX-daughter-in-law***!

Think about it though.

It is true.

Men ARE like buses.

Ok, so we have a regular bus (*man*) we like to ride, (*lol*), and one day we are heading to that same corner to wait for that good old dependable bus (*man*) to roll down the street toward us, and for some unforeseeable reason, we ***MISS*** the bus (*man*)!

The Dating Game

Now this could take the form of many causations here, remember this is an analogy. Maybe we broke it off, they broke it off, he didn't call, whatever...but we missed the bus (*man*).

So what to do?

Our first impulse is to begin running down the street after the bus (*man*) regardless of whether we are in our high heels or our Keds and try to catch that bus we just missed! What happens nine times out of ten when you chase a bus down the street?

You got it. Nothing. We end up out of breath and a block or so away from the stop where the next bus (*man*) will cruise by.

Most of us learn to calmly walk back to the bus (*man*) stop and just wait for the next bus (*man*) to come by. **MOST** of us.

Some of us are so obsessed with having that particular bus (*man*) that we may chase the bus for ten blocks, or, God forbid, all the way to our original destination! What happens then? Well, if we can run that far and have that much endurance, our feet will blister, we'll be disheveled and tired, and guess what? The bus (*man*) turns around and goes back the other way to continue its' route!

What happens if we just walk on back to the original bus (*man*) stop?

Just like my good old ex-mother-in-law said those many, many years ago...

Another bus (*man*) comes by.

Top Four Ways To Sabotage a Relationship

Women all over the United States tend to sabotage their relationships by falling into four basic traps, often brought about by our own misperceptions or insecurities.

When calling for a reading, a woman is quite frequently concerned with "where is this relationship going", a very valid question, which the cards will provide an answer to, provided the woman seeking the answer remains on the same path.

If the woman likes the answer she receives from the tarot, she need not (and should not) make any changes to her current path. If the woman seeking guidance does not like the answer, she may consult the cards again as to what, if anything, can be done to change the outcome of the reading to one that is more in line with her desires.

Sometimes an adjustment to her path can bring about the desired change. At other times the cards will advise the woman seeking knowledge that no significant improvement to the outcome can be made, it is out of her hands.

The most difficult answer to give a client is the one that he or she does not want to hear.

Often, these four factors come into play in sabotaging an otherwise promising relationship.

1. An incessant need to know "Where is this going?" and an aggressive approach to receiving this information direct from the horse's mouth. It takes men a lot longer to process their feelings than it does women. A woman may feel that this is the "right fit" with a man very early on, within weeks, whereas a man may take several months to sort out what he thinks and feels and actually know whether he wants this to "go anywhere" or not. Pressuring the man to engage in this conversation is much the same as pushing him away with all of

your might! He may come close again, but each time you bring this up, you are pushing him farther and farther away. Try to have a little patience, allow him the time required to decipher his own thoughts and feelings. The more you ask, the more resistant the man will become to answering. His actions speak louder than any words he can offer anyway. Is he consistent and attentive? If so, he wants this to continue to grow. Is he negligent and unthoughtful? Why would you want it to go anywhere with him anyway? There is no need to ask this question of him, pay attention to his actions.

2. Giving up your own identity and your own interests. If you were an active member of a book club, a chess club, enjoyed hang-gliding or sailing, arts and crafts, horseback riding, anything at all, and the moment you felt you were getting involved you abandoned these activities in order to focus your time and attention on him, you are well on your way to losing him. In my previously published blog, ***How Do YOU Like Your Eggs***?, this is discussed. Maintaining your interests and your individuality will continue to intrigue him. Becoming his shadow will make him feel smothered and he will ultimately become bored with the connection when you have nothing to bring to the relationship but a mirror image of himself.

3. Investing your interest and energy in a man that you believe you "can change". No one ever changes unless they want to. If you don't believe that you can accept him as he is, he is not the right guy for you. If you invest your time and energy in a man and believe that once you are committed you will change him, you are setting yourself up for a huge disappointment. If he likes to watch sports all day on a Sunday and you sit by and watch with him for six months, and then during month seven you begin to complain that all you do on Sundays is watch sports, you are not going to get him to turn off the TV and go parasailing with you.

He is going to tell you to go along and have fun parasailing, he'll be in front of the tube when you get back, and you are going to be angry. Don't accept anything that you don't find tolerable from the beginning. If it is an adjustment he is comfortable with, he will accommodate you quickly. If he is uncomfortable or stubborn about it, either accept it as part of him, or move on to someone who is a better match for you.

4.   Living for the future. This is definitely not healthy, as we all live in the present. If you are spending much of your time and energy focusing on some distant and imagined future, while experiencing a high level of dissatisfaction in the present, you are wasting your time. If you are not happy now, you are highly unlikely to be any happier in the future. This condition is often experienced when a woman is also afflicted by point 3, above, believing you can change him. If you aren't happy with who he is and how your relationship is **IN THE NOW**, you are setting yourself up to fail, and missing new opportunities by not moving on to a better match. There is nothing wrong with being happy and hoping for a deeper commitment in the future, but check and see, are you really happy now? If not, why do you think you'll be happier in the future? Why do you even want a commitment from a man who makes you unhappy?

So, when you call for a tarot reading, don't just ask what the potential for a given relationship is, or when is he going to call. Ask questions as to what the challenges you will face with this partner are. Get a feel for what obstacles you may encounter. Try to stay away from the saboteurs above and look at whether or not the obstacles that may arise between you are surmountable or not. Ask for what your best course of action is when interacting. Ask if there will be commitment issues. Ask if you will be compatible. Ask if he will treat you with respect. These are the issues to focus on at the beginning of a relationship, or during a "break" period. It is not as critical as to when he contacts you, as it is as to the degree of respect he will contact you with.

The Dating Game

Careful What You Wish For... You Just Might Get It!

Isn't it funny that when we **DON'T** have someone or something in our life, we idealize it to a point of obsession?

I can't tell you just how many times this has happened, but it happens with a fairly frequent occurrence.

I receive a call, or a series of calls, from a querent concerning a relationship that is **"On a Break"**.

The break may be a few weeks, a few months, or perhaps even stretch out into a year, no matter, when we read together, in some time frame, we see reconciliation.

The problem is...

During the "On a Break" phase, no matter how I try to cajole and coax the querent to use this time to comparison shop and **ENSURE** psychologically and emotionally that **THIS PERSON** is truly the best match for them and **WORTHY** of all this pain and suffering, they, (in the majority of cases), do not move on. They do not "*investigate other opportunities*" and remain obsessed with the ultimate return of the object of their affections.

The old saying "*Absence Makes the Heart Grow Fonder*" is true. It is frequently what makes the estranged lover return, and, conversely, is also likely to cause the jilted partner to idealize the absent partner in the wake of the break up.

So, now, when the jilted one speaks of the absent one, (and it usually gets worse with time), the sarcasm in the absent lovers' personality is viewed as wit, flirtatious behaviors become charming, disregard for their feelings becomes focus on career, etc. etc. etc. All of the faults that the absent partner possesses somehow magically are transformed into amazingly positive characteristics! How can they live without this love?! No one can ever make them feel like this ONE person does!!

This is the problem, during a break, the wisest thing to do is to let go as soon as possible and to begin moving forward. It is very difficult to do, (*I know, been there, done that, have the T-Shirt*), but it is the healthiest thing to do.

Let me explain why.

If, during your break, you do not put yourself out there to meet other potential mates, you run the risk of:

a)   Extending your period of mourning the relationship and causing yourself more pain, you have no distractions, all of your free time is spent examining your pain, feeling your pain, you are immobilized, you have to move to get the blood flowing again so that the wound can heal.

b)   Idealizing your current ex, who may very well be a scallywag that was not worthy of your affection and attention to begin with

c)   Miss opportunities to meet a new partner who will be a better match to you emotionally and psychologically

d)   Lose your "Partner Thermometer", and so idealize your ex that you get back into the original relationship with no new knowledge or level of understanding only to repeat the same mistakes over again. **THEN** realize that he or she was not the right person for you anyway.

Here are the benefits of getting out there and dating while on a break, or in any kind of "***Relationship Limbo***" for that matter:

a)   Your time is spent socializing and taking your mind off of your pain, thus helping you to begin to heal.

b)   You realize that others will treat you well and be attentive and that it feels good when someone actually seeks your company rather than flees from it.

c)   It gives you practice (as a woman), without emotional investment, in accepting or rejecting the way people treat you, or practice (as a man) of seeing yourself being respected and trusted…. See My Other Blogs on **_Masculine and Feminine Energy_**

d)   You don't have to **MARRY** the people you date in the interim, it teaches you how to date **CASUALLY** without heavy emotional or sexual involvement. You are dating at this time to be social and learn what other venues are available to you.

e)   You may actually meet someone who is a **BETTER MATCH** for you overall, thus resolving your break up issue and curing your painful condition

Whether you get back with your ex or not, you should never remain socially celibate during a break up.

Now, if and when you do reconcile and you **HAVE NOT** exercised your right to live freely during the break, you get back into the relationship with **NO NEW PERSPECTIVES** and an idealized vision of the current love. This puts you in a precarious position, because now your former ex may have the attitude of "I came back to you, what more do you want", and you gain no ground in your relationship and also no growth in the relationship.

You may then begin to realize that this isn't the partner for you after all, and that you have wasted not only the time spent mourning the break up, which may have been lengthy, but also the time spent reconciling, only to decide that now **YOU** want to end it. Believe it or not, in the cases where clients call me concerned about reconciliation, about 25% end up ending the relationship they pined for so desperately during the first year of reconciliation. It usually is not a "new issue" that makes the break occur, but old, unresolved issues, due to the fact that no growth occurred during the break period. Some feel that they have won a battle when the ex returns, only to lose the war and throw the relationship out with the next round of problems.

If, however, you **DO** take advantage of the time apart to expand your horizons, and you decide to re-enter the relationship, you are doing so with a clear vision, having been able to run a comparison and a reality check during your break.

Your odds for a successful reconciliation will go up dramatically once you have removed the rose-colored glasses by living fully outside of your relationship!

You then have a clear understanding of the original partner and can accept him or her as a real, flawed person, warts and all!

So, be careful what you wish for and use your time apart wisely to ensure a happy future.

Have You Performed a **_Relationship Autopsy_**?

The Dating Game

Doing the Relationship Limbo?

I **LOVE** to dance, oh Lord, how I love to dance, **but I hate doing the limbo.**

First of all, there is really no rhyme or reason to the damn dance, you bend over backwards trying to scrunch under a piece of bamboo, *(the enemy)*, perhaps weighed down by a heavy drink *(hehehe)*, and if you're lucky you don't fall flat on your arse!

Are you doing the **Relationship Limbo**?

Are you **dancing alone**?

Are you **bending over backwards** trying to get the object of your affections to reciprocate?

Every time you scrunch your butt under that bar, does he lower that rotten enemy bamboo **closer to the floor** while he raises the bar on some unidentified expectations of you in order to ask you to Tango?

Ooooh, **I love the Tango.**

It is the sexiest dance around as far as I am concerned.

First of all, you can't do it alone, you need **TWO!**

You don't have to be a contortionist either!

The masculine energy twirling you around the dance floor, pulling you with testosterone back into his strong, muscled arms, only to spin you out to the length of your two joined arms, and pulling you back again in a rush! In passion you slide down to the floor, and then he pulls you up, lifts you up, yes! Yes! Back into his manly arms!

Wouldn't you rather do the **Relationship Tango**?

I prefer it.

I had to learn how to take that stupid dance of standing in line and waiting to contort myself backwards under the bar and just leap over the enemy bamboo to the DJ and put a Tango CD in and **DANCE WITH MY PARTNER**!

No partner available?

No problem.

Plenty of men love to **"dance"**, just let them know you are available for a twirl and they will be more than happy to escort you around the dance floor. Your Tango may not be as passionate as it could be if it is not with the partner you truly desire, but you will learn to enjoy it!

Meanwhile, **Mr. Limbo**, can stand there all by himself with nothing in his hands but that stick!

Let's **TANGO**!

The Limbo is just too uncomfortable!

The Dating Game

On The Outside Looking In

"Your vision will become clear only when you look into your heart...

Who looks outside, dreams. Who looks inside, awakens."

Carl Jung

Frequently when under stress or in crisis a client will call and all of their questions will be focused on the object of their affections, concerns are projected outside, and the only *"inner"* focus is on how terrible they feel at present.

Of course, my position as a New Age Life Coach is to answer their questions as honestly and accurately as possible, and deliver even the negativity that may be energetically surrounding their situations as compassionately as possible.

The difficulty lies in trying to communicate to the client that they may very well need to remove their focus from the outside and switch it to the inside.

When in an emotional crisis, many are so focused on what may happen next or why their partner is behaving in a negative way, that it is very difficult to clearly deliver that message. Even when delivered kindly and gently, the client may not be able to hear what I am saying, dismissing the guidance that the cards are delivering to return to their focus questions of *"Why did he?"* and *"When will he?"*.

I am writing this Blog, *(and many previous Blogs),* as a gentle reminder or soft guidance to my clientele, that they may perhaps begin to change the focus of their concerns and questions from the outside to the inside.

The Dating Game

Let me give you some examples to ponder. Please remember that this is not directed toward any client or clients in particular, it is based on being a Professional Tarot Reader for ten years and providing over 35,000 readings in that timeframe, so if you see yourself in here, you are one of many I am writing this for.

Example Outward Focus Question:

Why did he break up with me?

Example Inward Focus Questions:

What was it in my behaviors that caused him to behave like this toward me? Am I needy? Am I clinging? Am I too strong for him?

How are his current behaviors making me feel?

Why do I allow him to make me feel this way?

How can I take control over my emotions and take "my power" back?

Example Outward Focus Question:

When will he call?

Example Inward Focus Question:

What can I do during this break to improve myself?

What was my contribution to this problem? What was his?

Why do I want him to call?

Why can't I let go and move on?

Example Outward Focus Question:

Will he come back to me?

Example Inward Focus Questions:

Do I really want him back?

What is it about him that makes me love him?

Do I love him or his potential?

Do I love him, or my projection of him?

What is it about him that makes me feel negative?

Example Outward Focus Question:

How does he feel about me right now?

Example Inward Focus Question:

How do I truly feel about him?

Example Outward Focus Question:

What will make him come back to me?

Example Inward Focus Question:

Do I really want him back?

The Dating Game

Sometimes when our relationships hit crisis points or breakup it is more upsetting to us because the rhythm of our lives has changed and we now have a new path before us. We outwardly focus on the absent partner not because we truly love them, but because we were comfortable in our routines and the disruption to those routines is very ominous.

If you have to move out, you don't know where you are going to live just yet. If you have had a long-term relationship your circle of friends may very well change, you suddenly find you have weekends with nothing to do except focus on your loss when you could be making plans to do things you always wanted to do but never got around to.

I listen daily to people talk about their exes and ask outwardly focused questions about them as exemplified above. There are occasions when the client combines the outward with the inward and realizes that they truly are in love with their estranged partner. They do the work required to heal their relationship, and sometimes that work entails a lengthy separation and a life on a totally separate path for awhile, but these are the clients who do go inward as well as outward.

What is difficult is to hear clients focus outward and feel their desperation at regaining their lost love, but then also listen to them quantify all of the faults of their estranged partner, which prompts me to ask, are you sure that you want them back? How do you really feel about him? By doing so, I try to steer them inward, but few follow the map.

In my Blog, ***"Careful What You Wish For, You Just Might Get It"*** I share with you some insights into a frequent occurrence post-reconciliation within my client base, if you are in the midst of a breakup right now you may also wish to read and consider that particular Blog as well.

"Happiness, not in another place, but this place...

Not for another hour, but this hour."

Walt Whitman

The Dating Game

He Chased Me Until I Caught Him!

LOL!

That is what Frank always says about how we ended up getting together over thirteen years ago.

It's a long, long story. Some of my regulars who have formed a deep working relationship with me through the Life Coaching Process are well aware of it, as, when appropriate, I have cited examples from a decade of trials and tribulations.

Some Advisors do not feel it is appropriate to use personal experience in order to counsel others. I happen to believe that it is an integral part of the Life Coaching Process. Personally, *I don't give credence* to anyone who offers me advice or counsel unless they have had some experience with a like situation themselves.

Oh, if you are just calling me for a "Quickie Psychic Reading", I will accommodate you, but the clients who benefit the MOST from my service are clients who are seekers of not only a predictive reading, but also counsel on how to best navigate their current course. These are the clients who ultimately make the most extensive progress and are most likely to achieve their goals.

Anyway, throughout our lengthy history, I have learned a lot. I suffered a lot too, when I didn't follow the natural energies of the male/female relationship. There were times when I totally succumbed to my masculine energies and hit a lot of hard challenges when I did.

How the ultimate success of our relationship unfolded was when I truly self-disciplined myself to stay in the primary energy role of the feminine. This doesn't mean that you play games, it is a conscious choice that you make, and for a Type A Personality like myself, whose natural primary energy is masculine, this was no mean feat. It was hard!!!

Now that we have **true commitment**, we are able to change back and forth between all four of our combined energies, but I still pay close attention to when they start to go off balance, and then evoke the primary energy necessary to put us back on balance. It is hard work.

One of the things we all must remember is that reaching the level of a **true commitment**, like marriage, is not the end all and be all, it is not the "goal" as my title suggests, it is the **beginning of the next stage** of our lives.

No more is it a simple task to severe the tie, now neither one of us can just say, "I want to break up" and walk away without going through the complexities and hassles of disentangling our connection through divorce. It is a lot harder to get out of a marriage than it is to get into one, and being a second marriage for both of us, we have our own specific set of challenges to face since we have tied this knot.

We both have children. We both have exes. We both have plenty of baggage.

The good thing is, we are both aware of it, so the only baggage that gets into our energy is our "carry-on baggage", like the fact that my youngest son still lived at home when we married. Yes, that is baggage, but it is carry-on because Frank understood that it was a package deal in that respect. This was not "excess baggage" that you pay a fee to tote along with you, like resentment toward your first spouse might be.

So, although I am very happy about the life changes I have made, I have done so with full awareness that this is not the end of the journey, just the beginning of the next leg.

It is funny, though, when Frank says "*He chased me until I caught him*", because in effect, utilizing your feminine energies causes just that phrase to occur!

Chapter Three

More Transitioning

The Dating Game

The Greatest Mistake of Women Through All Time

Ever wonder why....

....

Just a little tidbit of a thought that came to mind today.............

Forgive a Man his ways, and take responsibility for them.

....

The biggest mistake of Women through all time.

My mother did it, your mother probably did it, I did it in my past as well.

Why do we do it?

Because we so want the Man in our life to "come true".

The only way the Man we love will "come true", is if we, as the women in their lives, stay true to ourselves and reject bad behavior, not condone, overlook or accept it.

Think about it tonight while you may well be making an excuse for him as to why he hasn't called, or why he doesn't commit.

When we begin to fervently *REJECT* bad behavior, the Men in our lives begin to "come true".

Self Forgiveness, a Path to Inner Peace

Guilt is a heavy burden to carry around.

We have all done wrong in our lifetimes. Not one among us is without "sin", but do you let your past mistakes and transgressions haunt you, or are you able to forgive yourself and let go?

If you lay in bed at night and think of the past and a painful memory of something you did that caused another pain surfaces, are you able to look beyond it and get some rest that night? Or do you ruminate, run it through your head over and over and build that sick feeling in the pit of your abdomen, robbing yourself of sleep.

Few of us are able to forgive ourselves easily. The narcissist is likely the only personality type that has no issue with self forgiveness as they are only concerned with when others will seek their forgiveness, as they can only see how others hurt them.

Barring the fact that we suffer from a narcissistic personality, how do we begin to forgive ourselves and lay our past sins to rest?

First, we must acknowledge that we have done wrong, project ourselves into the emotions of the person or persons we may have knowingly or unknowingly damaged, including ourselves. Allow yourself to empathetically feel the pain that they may have felt and acknowledge to ourselves that it was wrong to put another human being into that state of emotional distress.

We do not try to justify our actions in any way, we simply feel their pain.

Now, we look at what we could have or should have done differently given that situation were to be duplicated. Odds are that in retrospect we have gained much clarity and can see how perhaps a different course of action or no action at all would have been a better path.

The Dating Game

We are not looking for excuses for our poor behavior, however, we should look at the person we were at the time the incident occurred and compare it to the person we are now. We may want to gain some psychological insight into our behavior by considering our state of mind, our age, our level of intent to cause harm, our emotional state and so forth, remember, we are not trying to justify our actions, we are simply trying to gain an understanding of them.

Once we are clearly able to identify the dynamics of the incident we must allow ourselves to heal, yes heal, guilt damages us from the inside just as much as outside influences affect us when inflicted in a negative way.

Now that we have accepted our wrongdoing and understand it a little better, we can forgive ourselves and let go, bringing ourselves to true "Inner Peace". We can look back, see the error of our ways, and move forward without our burden of guilt holding us back emotionally or psychologically.

It need not matter whether the person or persons we have harmed forgive us from the outside, at times, others may need to hold onto their anger. What matters is that we have forgiven ourselves.

How Speeding Things Up Can Slow Things Down

So, again, as in my blog, "***I Want It All, and I Want It Now!***", I'd like to discuss how a woman taking action to "speed up" their relationships actually slows things down in the big picture.

There are days when I am inundated with calls from clients who are in a relationship situation where they are "on a break" with the man that they care for.

This is not uncommon.

Frequently, relationships need to have periods where there is a clean break, in order for the male in question to experience life without you, in order to truly appreciate life **WITH** you.

Sometimes it's not even on a break, so to speak, but it's initiating contact, and the female can't wait for him to initiate, so she does it herself.

For the purpose of this particular blog, let's talk about the "Break" situation.

For some reason, including but not limited to any of the following reasons; "I don't have time for a relationship right now", "I am not ready for a relationship right now", "Let's keep it as friends", "I have to focus on career, school, my kids, my divorce, etc.", the man in your life has called it off. Perhaps you were the one to call it off because your needs were not being met, but now, you want the relationship back.

It hurts.

You love him.

You feel abandoned.

You feel a sense of internal panic without the consistency of him in your life.

You cry.

You want him to change his mind and come back.

You aren't sure what to do.

You call an advisor for some insight and some advice or reassurance. You want to see if the Tarot Cards can clue you in as to what is going on inside him and as to what he will likely do about your relationship in the future.

You are not alone.

You need to talk to someone and get a handle on the situation.

There is absolutely nothing wrong with experiencing this. You are a caring, feeling human being, and the feelings you are experiencing right now are unpleasant to say the least, and they are also very distracting, making it hard for you to focus on other areas of your life.

So, you get a reading and you are going to get an answer in one of two directions, either (a) the gentleman in question is not coming back and the break is going to be a permanent one, or (b) he is going to realize that he misses you and get in touch with his feelings for you and return.

If your answer is (a), it hurts, but hearing it from an experienced and compassionate advisor may help you to let go, heal, and subsequently move on.

If your answer is (b), you feel a bit better, but, in 9 out of 10 cases, your next question will be "When?".

This is usually where the female querent gets a bit frustrated. ***Timing with the Tarot*** is exceptionally difficult.

Unless the woman is the one who broke the relationship and did something hurtful, it is usually best to allow the male to work through his feelings and allow him to initiate the contact leading toward reconciliation.

Why?

It's usually best because this way, when he returns, he returns without any doubt of what he wants, he has made the decision himself and he is likely to be more committed upon his return than he ever was before.

So, what happens if the female tries to speed things up?

Well, in varying degrees she may be unsuccessful and push him farther away, delaying reconnecting or disallowing it all together if she is too intense in her pursuit, or, she can actually cause the reconnection to occur sooner.

If she is successful, the problem is, the success is generally short-lived or temporary.

When a break occurs, it occurs for a reason. If you do not allow the male to work through whatever his issues or doubts were in his own time, they will resurface and you are highly likely to experience the break cycle again, often more severe, and possibly permanently.

His return happens because you pushed for it, not because he chose to return on his own.

Now he knows that he can break up with you and not truly sacrifice his relationship with you because you will be there for him the next time he gets ants in his pants.

The Dating Game

You may get the "immediate gratification" of putting things back together, but your foundation is not solid, it is built on your actions, not his. He is back, but now he knows that he's not risking losing you if he leaves again because you have taught him that you will chase him if he does.

Now, in the event that you do wait it out, it may take weeks or even months longer to reconcile. However, when he does come back to you of his own free will, without your pushing and pulling him to you, he will most likely be more committed to you because he did lose you and you were gone, and you put the "work" in his lap. He will realize how close he came to losing you permanently, and allowing him to work through whatever feelings of ambivalence about your connection he had has allowed him to truly commit to you and the relationship. He will be unlikely to leave again.

Waiting out this process is very difficult for many of us of the feminine persuasion.

We want our man back in our life and worry and pine over them during these breaks. This is normal when you care about someone, but it is in the best interest of the relationship overall if you can just communicate to him very simply "I wish things were different, but I understand your decision, take care", and let go.

Many of us feel incapable of doing so. We want it, and we want it now, so we don't follow this advice and we contact them and we pour our hearts out, and we may very well get them back, but we get them back on their terms, not ours, frequently with even less of a commitment than we had before. We then become so afraid of losing them again that we tolerate poor behavior, missed phone calls, lack of attention to our needs and postponements for dates, etc.

We may feel that rush of accomplishment at having "won him back" initially, but it is usually quickly followed by a sense of frustration. Perhaps, then even more phone calls to an advisor, asking questions such as "when will he call, when will he commit". While, if we had just let him work through his feelings and let go when we had the chance we would have gotten a strong return from him with consistency in communications and a deeper level of commitment to our relationship.

So, if you are finding yourself on a break and wondering what you should do, if you are not the one who did the "breaking", do nothing. Let him work through his feelings. Move forward. Socialize, date others, let him know you wish that things were different before you do move on without him, but move forward just the same. It is difficult, but you will find that if you are not focused on his return you will feel better and you will also find that he will miss you more in the absence of your energy and he will return more quickly and with a renewed sense of value for you and your relationship.

If you push for a premature reconnection and you successfully achieve it, you must be aware that within six to eight weeks or sooner you are likely to be repeating a pattern of his pulling away or breaking off with you.

So, immediate gratification or long-term satisfaction, is it worth the wait to you?

Surviving an Affair

Is it possible to salvage a relationship when your loved one has been untrue?

Yes, anything is possible, however, this particular possibility is a very difficult one.

First and foremost, you have been hurt, deeply hurt.

No one understands the depth of how much pain an unfaithful spouse or lover can bring to a tender heart more than one who has been through it, and I feel for all who have experienced this particular hell, I've been there myself.

In order for your relationship to successfully get past this point and move forward once again, we must be able to forgive the transgression.

This is very, very difficult, and for some of us, it is an exercise in futility. An inability to forgive this trespass will poison any attempts at truly reconciling the issue. It is very difficult to forgive someone who has inflicted this level of pain on us, and truthfully, some of us are not capable of this level of forgiveness.

Prior to beginning to work on your relationship again, you must first truly examine whether or not you are able to forgive your partner for being unfaithful. Be honest with yourself, this is a key factor in regaining the love you once had for this partner.

All affairs are different. Some are just sexual, some are emotional, and some are just a one night stand. What type of an affair did your partner partake in? Personally, I was more hurt by the fact that my partner became (or risked becoming) emotionally involved than by the sexual or physical aspects of an affair, but everyone is different.

Self Examination.

Are you going to be able to put this out of your mind? Are you ever going to be able to trust your partner again? Is your partner truly willing to be faithful and exclusive to you emotionally and physically from this point on?

Answers to YOUR Questions.

You need to sit down with your partner and ask the painful questions, was it sex, was it love, was it a way out, or was it just a fling? The answers from your partner need to be honest and open, and your partner must feel that you are not going to rip their head off if they tell you the truth in order to feel safe enough to be honest about it.

Is The Affair Over?

Your partner must agree to have absolutely no further contact with the person they cheated with. This, in some cases, can be extremely difficult, especially if the straying spouse had an affair with a coworker and they both still work together. It may warrant your partner changing jobs if this is economically feasible, as unless all contact ceases and desists, you may have an unusually difficult time regaining trust in the fallen partner.

Is Your Partner Sensitive to Your Feelings?

You will be angry, hurt, distrustful, upset and confused as you begin this process. It is an emotional roller coaster that no one wants to be on. In order to survive, your partner needs to be empathetic to your feelings (which may last for years after the affair), and respect and nurture your need for extra effort to reestablish trust.

Taking Responsibility

Both you and your partner must take responsibility for the actions and interactions between you that led up to the affair. No, I am not blaming the innocent partner here, but affairs happen because something is lacking in a relationship.

The Dating Game

You must dive down into the depths of your original relationship and examine the root causes of this infidelity. In some cases, the wayward partner is just a pure schmuck, in that case, why do you want them back? But in most instances, something was missing that caused the affair. Identify it and fix it. If it is irreparable, you may not be able to salvage your relationship.

Communicate, Communicate, Communicate

No one wants to beat a dead horse, but surviving an affair can actually bring the two of you closer together and give you the ability to be more honest with each other than you ever have been before. Of course, the preferred state of being is to never have to deal with an infidelity in the first place, however, it happens. If you choose to survive it, you can, but you must communicate effectively with each other in order to prevent any further mishaps from occurring and to truly have a new beginning in each other's lives.

Have You Any Stalking Tendencies?

Can't Let Go?

Take This Test To See....

Are You a Stalker?

We get interested in men, we get frustrated, at times, by men, we get hurt by men, we fall in love with men, and we break up and make up with men. In the complicated world of relationships, we ride the rollercoaster of *masculine and feminine energy* and we, at times, fall prey to our weaker instincts and do things that we normally would not do as rational, adult women.

Respond to these statements honestly, yes or no.

Results will be given at the bottom of this little quiz to see if you have ever been a "*stalker*", or are having a hard time letting go of a person.

1. You have blocked your number and dialed a man's phone number and immediately hung up, just to hear his voice and get a "*rush*". *(You may have then spent hours or days analyzing his tone of voice and/or the background noises present during that split second call).*

2. You have logged onto match or myspace or facebook under a pseudo name just to check his profile and any activity on his account.

3. You have gone out of your way to do "*drive-by's*" past his work, his home, and his haunts just to see if there have been any changes in his movements or habits.

4. You know his movements and habits so well that if he is not at any of the places listed in Item 3, above, you panic when he is not within his normal routine.

5. You have accessed his cell phone account and looked up every number he has called through the web and those that you could not identify, you rang, as in Item 1 above.

6. You have actually spent time trying to crack his password on his email, voicemail, myspace, facebook or match account.

7. You show up at his "*usual*" haunts trying to behave as if you would be there "*anyway*", but you know, in reality, you are only there in the hopes of bumping into him and creating an interaction that would not otherwise occur.

8. You have run a "*background*" check on him through the web to try to pin down any information about him that you may not have already gathered, and you paid good money for it.

9. You pump any mutual friends or acquaintances that you have for information, in what you believe is a seemingly "*casual*" way, and subsequently follow up on any "*leads*" you may get as to his current activity.

10. You have conducted your own "*stake-out*" of his home, work place, or favorite haunts.

Here are your scores

If you answered yes to statement 1, you are not alone. This is a common practice among American Women of all ages, and can easily be explained away as a Freudian slip, or an accidental dial. Repeatedly indulging in statement one behavior, however, can indicate a problem.

If you answered yes to statement 2, you're still in the realm of the average curiosity level of the American Female, although the information you gain by doing so may only serve to hurt your feelings.

The Dating Game

If you answered yes to number 3, you are starting to get a little bit higher onto the Stalker Scale of possessiveness, and plotting his movements in this manner is wasting your time and feeding your obsession. You really should go out of your way to not drive by these locations.

A combination of items one, two and three is beginning to put you into stalker mode, and you really should try to stop.

If you answered yes to number 4, you are climbing the Stalker Scale and hurting yourself more than anyone. Stop here. The only thing that will happen with this knowledge is that you will hurt yourself.

If you answered yes to number 5, you are well on your way to topping out on the Stalker Scale. You are invading his privacy and could well face criminal charges if you get caught. Stop immediately. Let go.

If you answered yes to number 6, you are on a path to self-destruction, and if caught, again, you could face criminal charges and public humiliation. Please stop.

If you answered yes to number 7, you are in "*chase*" mode with this man, and the only thing that your presence and persistence will do is make the man react by pulling farther away. It is true that absence makes the heart grow fonder. Putting yourself squarely in his path at every opportunity is **NOT** going to make him realize that he misses you and that he wants more with you. Your elusiveness will do more to fan his flames of desire more than anything else.

Answering yes to number 8 is pure stalking, you are not going to find any sense of relief or gratification in the information that you find. Let go.

If you answered yes to number 9, you are being blatantly obvious, and again, you are in chase mode.

Answering yes to number 10 indicates that you are at risk of having a restraining order placed against you, if the male in question is so inclined, and you are running the risk of discovery.

Count up your answers to the positive. On a scale of one to ten, the higher your score, the more obsessive your behavior. Love can lead to madness, but there is no need to torture yourself and risk criminal charges over a male whose behavior drives you to such lengths.

If you score a zero, you a very healthy and secure woman, and probably had no interest in even reading this blog.

If you score one to three, you are exhibiting insecurity on a level that is about average when a relationship is not progressing as you would like.

If you score three to six, you are beginning to exhibit signs of obsession and should really examine this relationship and how it is hurting you, not adding to your life, but reducing the quality of your life.

If you score above six, you are in danger of losing yourself and your self-esteem by placing your focus on an outside source for gratification and you need to begin to look inside. You are also in danger of having criminal charges placed against you should the person you are doing this to feel that you have violated their privacy in this manner.

Rather than spending time and energy in these ill-fated pursuits, try moving forward and living the life that you have always imagined yourself living. Pick up a new hobby, pick up a new man, redefine yourself, change your style, and focus on yourself and not this person on the outside who is being so inattentive as to cause you to behave a bit irrationally.

The Dating Game

Chapter Four

Breaking Up

The Dating Game

Should I Stay or Should I Go Now?

Many clients call and have concerns because their relationships are not *"perfect"*, and some may be striving for the *"next level"* and frustrated with what they perceive as a lack of progress.

Perhaps they have been dating the same gentleman for 2 years and he has not yet proposed, or perhaps they are living together and he has not yet asked for marriage, or perhaps they are casually dating and he has not yet asked to be *"exclusive"* or defined the relationship at a level they are satisfied with, i.e. significant other.

Well, let me start by telling you that as a New Age Life Coach, it would be totally unethical and unprofessional for me to tell you **WHAT to do**. The best counsel I can offer you is what you can expect given your current path and what changes you would need to make if you are dissatisfied with the outcome. The rest is up to you, your free will will define the course as you move forward. If you like the outcome, of course, you are going to stay on that same path working toward that goal. If you do not like the outcome, we can look at what (if anything) you can do to change that particular outcome...and work from there.

One of the primary reasons that progress slows in relationships prior to establishing the *"next level"* of commitment, no matter what step of the relationship ladder you are on, is the imbalance of masculine and feminine energies within a pairing. Please read my blogs on the subject matter for further information.

If you love the person you are with, my best advice to you is to try to rectify the relationship you are in first, to the best of your ability, prior to breaking it off and starting from scratch again. Unless you are in an abusive situation, in which case you should end it immediately, it is best to repair the cracks in your existing foundation prior to tearing the whole relationship down.

Starting over is always a bit of a setback when you are looking for a committed relationship as you have to start from ground zero all over again, shop around, test them out, it takes time, a lot of time, and you already have a certain amount of time invested in your current situation.

If you have been dating casually and you want to know how long it should take to become exclusive, the answer varies, and you have to take into consideration whether or not you have allowed physical intimacy to take place absent the *"exclusivity"* clause. If you have had physical relations prior to establishing your exclusiveness, you've got a bit of a situation on your hands as you have already communicated the message to your partner that you are willing to give of yourself in that manner without any commitment from him, it's a tough one.

If you have been exclusive and dating for some time, how long should it take for him to propose? There is no standard answer or timeframe for that question. Every individual has their own *"commitment clock"* and I would be remiss to answer that. The issue is, **how much time are you willing to invest in a relationship prior to engagement and marriage?**

If you are not happy with your relationship clock, then you cannot force him to commit. The only thing you can do is tell him that you wish that things were different, but you are ready for a deeper commitment and if he is not willing to make that commitment to you, you need the freedom to find someone who is on the same time schedule as you. Then you must exit the situation.

If he really loves you, he won't let you go for long, he may take a few months, and you may need to move on, but if he really loves you, he will come back and commit.

Should you stay or should you go?

Most people are afraid to endure the pain to effect change by risking loss, but loss can be turned into gain. You can turn your current situation around by risking loss, or you can find a new situation that does not require so much analysis when you actually do **take matters** *into your own hands and reject situations that are unsatisfactory to you.*

Denial Is NOT a River In Egypt

A Journey Into New Age Life Coaching

Coping With a Break Up

In my professional practice, this is a nearly constant subject of discussion with clients.

As my **Life Coaching** is based in **New Age Philosophies** of **Tarot, Astrology** and the **Metaphysical**, at times it is difficult to get a client to focus on ways to cope with the situation at hand, as their focus is on the **Psychic Implications** of their sessions more than on the **Here and Now** of surviving this difficult period.

Questions typically focus on *"Will He Come Back"*, *"When Will He Call"*, *"Is He With Someone Else"*, *"Why Did He Do This"*, etc.

These are questions that I will answer to the best of my ability through the **Professional Interpretation of the Tarot Cards.**

I consider this Step One of my Advisor Sessions.

Many clients do not consider Step Two, either because they are accustomed to working with advisors who may not offer a *"Step Two"*, or, because they are so overcome by their situation that they cannot release their focus from the predictive stage of my coaching process due to their internal pain.

So, I felt that I would write a blog about Step Two, this is the *"Life Coaching"* portion of my professional practice and although Tarot, Astrology and other Metaphysical Methods may be employed during this process, for the most part, it is a very mainstream approach.

In coping with a break up, there are several things you must consider and try to stay aware of while you heal. Whether or not the individual in question will return is irrelevant, this is about taking care of **YOU** and making sure that you cope with your break up as well as is possible.

These processes may well get us into deeper issues that bring us back to using Tarot and Astrology et al to examine them further.

First of all, a reality check is in order.

What do I mean by that?

Well, your level of emotional response to the break up should not be disproportionate to the level of relationship that you had.

If you had an extensively lengthy relationship or marriage, naturally you are going to be very upset. You may possibly be clinically depressed if you are prone to an imbalance of serotonin in your biology, and you should go to your regular physician for a check up to be certain that you are not experiencing any physical side effects from your emotional trauma.

If you experience any of the following, you really need to see your doctor: *insomnia, "oversleeping", fatigue, lack of appetite, markedly increased appetite, inability to focus, emotionally charged outbursts, including but not limited to crying jags, rages, etc., disinterest in the day to day details of life (like not opening your mail or paying your bills),* etc. All of these may interfere with your normal daily functioning and may well be symptoms of *clinical depression*.

Paying medical attention to yourself during this period is extremely important and I frequently recommend that my clients get a physical during this period from their medical professional.

Ok, so you dragged yourself out of the house and you took care of the medical side of your "*condition*", you may have even found that your doctor recommended professional counseling from a licensed medical professional and you have also taken care of that. Good.

Now, what can you expect?

Well, honestly, if you really cared about the person you are going to go through many stages, not in any specific order, but just like grieving a death, you must allow yourself to grieve this relationship, and you will experience the *Five Stages of Grief*:

Denial   *(NOT a River in Egypt) "This CAN'T be HAPPENING"*

Anger   *Why me? How could he/she do this to me? It's not fair!*

Bargaining   *Just give me one more chance*

Depression   *I can't go on without my partner*

Acceptance   *Life will go on whether he comes back or not*

Quite frankly, at the acceptance stage is usually when the break up comes to resolution, either the lover returns or the client moves on.

In my practice, I encourage and guide my clients toward acceptance whenever I can.

Acceptance is arriving at a level of healing, and that same release of energy will allow an estranged lover to return. It is the preferred state of existence after a breakup.

Unfortunately, there are times when a client gets caught up in one of the other four stages of grief and cannot get to the stage of acceptance.

The most frequently stalled stage of grief is Denial.

Speaking in terms of timing to reach the level of acceptance, it is not unusual for it to take a proportionate amount of time to the length of the relationship to reach acceptance, and to continuously cycle through the other four stages of grief during this process.

The Dating Game

A good *"**Rule of Thumb**"* for *"**Timing to Acceptance**"* is one month for each year that you were involved with your partner. So if you were involved for six years, expect it to take an approximate six months to heal, if you were dating for a brief period, the same rule applies. If you were dating for six months or less, you should be able to reach acceptance in about a two week to one month period.

If your relationship was less than two months, you should be able to reach acceptance in an approximate two week period.

What does it mean if you are not reaching the acceptance level in a time frame proportionate to your relationship length?

Well, this frequently means that you are hung up in the stage of ***Denial**.

This is a dangerous place to be because if you are stuck here, you may well not be paying attention to the fact that you may also be experiencing some degree of clinical depression, and again, you should seek the counsel of your medical professional. This is the same as having the card of *The Hanged Man* crowning you. You are stagnant, just staying where you are and waiting for things to change rather than taking steps to progress yourself through your grief.

This is frequently when clients will seek the advice of a *Psychic Advisor*, and if the Advisor or Advisors are not chosen carefully, the client may find themselves prolonging their stagnation in denial.

It is no coincidence that the average timeframes for healing directly coincide with the potential timeframes for reconciliation.

If you have not reconciled with your lover or spouse during these suggested timeframes, it is extremely unlikely that reconciliation will occur.

This is where the *"reality check"* comes in.

How serious was your relationship to begin with?

Were you married for several (or many) years?

Were you living together for any length of time?

Were you dating for a year or so?

Were you dating for a few months?

Was it a brief, casual affair?

Was it "just a hook up"?

Really and truly, you must examine what the nature of the relationship in question was and look inward to see how realistically you are coping with the end of it.

Not all estranged lovers and spouses reunite and at the same time, not all breakups are permanent.

Each case is individual.

The danger of being caught in the stage of **Denial** when consulting Metaphysical or Psychic Advisors is that due to your state of **Denial** you may only be hearing what you want to hear, and you may be being drawn only to Advisors that you sense will tell you what you want to hear. This can cause what some refer to as a "**psychic junkie**" or "**psychic addiction**" syndrome. This can lead to financial problems, frustration and even misdirected rage if not avoided.

A "**psychic junkie**" or "**psychic addict**" is one who continuously calls a great number of psychics, repeatedly getting readings in the hopes of finding relief. They are reinforcing their **Denial**, to the point that they have maxed out their credit cards and may be having troubles meeting their other financial obligations due to their overuse of the services and their inability to stop validating their **Denial**.

The Dating Game

How can you tell if you are stuck in **Denial** and fueling it?

Well, do you avoid calling Advisors who are truly professional in nature and offer more than the psychic quick fix readings?

Do you only ask questions such as *"Is he coming back and when"*, rather than, *"What is in my best interest at this time in regard to this situation"*, for fear of being told you need to let go and move on?

Do you seek increasingly extreme metaphysicians? Like the **Witch**, the **Warlock**, the **Psychic** who uses *"No Tools"*? Rather than someone who is a **New Age Life Coach**, who offers more than a purely psychic interpretation of your situation, but advises you on a deeper level? Are you looking for a magickal answer to your dilemma? You're feeding your denial if you are.

There is nothing wrong with seeking this type of counsel, but try to balance it with the services of a person like myself, who is at a halfway point between mainstream life coaching and metaphysical service, to ensure that you are getting a fully rounded view of your circumstances.

It is very difficult to tell a person who is stalled in **Denial** that the object of their affections is not returning, but it must be done. The best interest of the client is to help them move toward acceptance to expedite their healing so that they can move forward to a new, healthier situation.

Even when the **Tarot Cards** definitively show that a person is returning to a client's life, I **STILL** encourage them to move toward **Acceptance.**

Why?

Because this empowers the client.

This allows the client to clearly see whether or not the estranged love is truly worthy of their attention and affection, this gives the client choices.

So, to continue, in coping with a breakup, I am advising you to take care of your physical health, and to try to ensure that you are not getting held up in the stage of *Denial.*

In my practice, when I find that a client is caught in *Denial*, I do identify it to them, gently and compassionately, and this is where the *Life Coaching* begins.

Through the use of Tarot and Astrology we begin to try to raise our *Anger*, not in the sense of being *Angry* for the loss of the love, but *Anger* in the sense of recognizing whatever wrongs the lost love may have done to our person, and feel that righteous *Anger*.

Many times, we idealize a lost lover, we look at them through rose colored spectacles rather than in the clear light of day. So we drag out the lost lover, warts and all, and we see what we need to see, together, in order to advance the process.

We then move toward *Bargaining,* not in the sense of "*giving anything*" to get them back, but in a more mature sense, *Bargaining* to gain clarity as to whether or not this person is even the "*right fit*" for the client. It may include having the client make a list of positives and negatives about the relationship as it was or the individual who is absent, etc., *Bargaining = Weighing.*

At this point, we are well on our way to the *Acceptance Stage*.

The clients that truly blossom with me and find my services the most useful, are the clients who are willing to look deeper into their situation, with the use of Tarot and Astrology, and come to terms (*Acceptance*), with their situations.

The journey to Acceptance is a difficult one, and it does *NOT* mean that you are "*giving up*" or "*abandoning all hope*". It means that you are going to position yourself for the healthiest possible outcome to your current condition. Acceptance, in psychological terms, is a realization that a situation cannot be changed or manipulated in order to ease your pain or suffering. Acceptance means you acknowledge that the situation is not what you wish it to be, working through the pain of that realization, healing and moving forward.

It is not a journey that you need to embark on alone.

Hate is NOT the Opposite of Love

What?

Hate IS the opposite of Love you say?

I disagree. Vehemently.

Hate and Love have too many similarities. The primary similarities are that both emotions require an intense energy and both emotions take time to develop and to expend.

When we hate someone, it is usually an extension of an anger that is burning within us, or a feeling that one of the conditions of being entitled to our love has not been met. Striving to love unconditionally is learning to let go of hate, anger and resentment.

The opposite of Love is not Hate, it is Apathy.

Think about it.

When we fall out of love with someone, when the love has truly run it's cycle, we begin the process of "*not caring*", not focusing, and not being attentive to what that individual is going through.

In Hate, the object of our admonitions is likely to get much of our attention and energy.

I have to say that during the times in my life when I truly fell "*out of Love*", I did not hate the person, not at all, I just did not want to affiliate or interact with them any longer. I wanted to move on, and although I did not necessarily want to hurt them, I did want to extinguish the bond between us.

In my younger years, I was actually very irresponsible about this. I would pull a "*disappearing act*", change my circle of friends and socialize in places where I knew the object of my apathy would not expect me to be or seek me. I changed my phone numbers and never responded to their attempts at connecting. I was not unkind when ending a relationship, it's just that I did it like a lightning bolt. Once I decided I was done, I was done, and began to immediately move on, there was no lingering.

This may have been painful for my new ex's over the years, however, it prompted them to give up and move on quickly, with my blessings, by the way. I am, to this day, still friends with each and every one of my ex's, with the exception of my ex-husband, and I don't hate him, I just don't wish to imbibe in the friendship of the man for reasons I will explain someday.

In retrospect, I should have taken my time with these jilted boyfriends and explained to them why I needed to end our connection in a kind manner. It would have meant more work for me, but less negative Karma later on. To this end, I have, in later years, explained myself to these gentlemen and rekindled friendships and been forgiven.

On the other hand, in the instances where I have hated an individual, *(quite frankly, it has never been a love, it has been a female friend or two that evoked this feeling in me)*, it was usually boiled down to a feeling that I had been betrayed by that individual.

The "*hates*" of my life were people I once cared deeply for and in essence, by hating them, I still did. In each case, it was because of the hurt I perceived they had laid on me.

In recent years, as I have matured, I have learned that my hate is not only non-productive, but also very draining to my overall energy, affecting my health and well-being. So what I have done is become very practiced in the art of forgiveness. I try to look at those I felt the emotion of hate for and examine the situations from their side of the coin. At times, you just have to accept that some people are just not as evolved as others and forgive them for their shortcomings. If they had intentionally hurt me, I also try to forgive them. I try to understand that they may have knowingly hurt me, but are as yet, too self-centered to have the realization of the karma they are putting upon their own souls, and wish that they grow into a better understanding of how each and every action produces a reaction in the universe, either actively or passively. I have even taken responsibility for situations I unwittingly caused or allowed to grow negative, and forgiven myself. I have sought forgiveness through apology and deed in cases where I could.

God and the Universe will take care of doling out whatever lessons they need to learn, just as my lessons have been sent my way. I just "**give it up to God**", and let Karma play itself out, and remove my energy and attention away from these individuals and allow apathy to replace the love I once carried for them.

Hate eats you up inside, it keeps you from moving forward, it burns your energy and wastes your time. Don't worry about how someone has hurt you to the point of wasting your time. Instead, focus your energy on growing in a better and healthier way toward understanding human nature. We are highly fallible beings, and the best that we can hope for is to hurt each other in as limited ways as possible and to have the opportunity to love as many people as we can while we are here.

Hate is not the opposite of Love, Hate is Love in its angriest, ugliest form.

When I die, I want a **LOT** of people to attend my services, as I believe the greatest exit from this life will be one in which everyone feels "*She was well-loved, and she knew how to love*".

Just a little reflection from the mind of Brigid Bishop.

When the One We Love Is With Someone Else

Nothing is more painful than being fully aware that the one we love is involved with someone else. It can manifest in many ways, we may find out that our loved one was unfaithful or we may be *"on a break"* and they are investigating other opportunities, or it may be conclusively over and they are moving on.

Regardless of the circumstances, it hurts and we suffer and grieve.

I always recommend that when any of us are suffering this type of emotional turmoil that we are sure to watch for signs of clinical depression and to seek professional medical help if we suspect we may be afflicted.

Now, how do we deal with it?

You must examine the reality of what type of a relationship you had in the first place. Was it a friendship, an infatuation, were you just dating casually, were you boyfriend and girlfriend for a few months, were you involved for a few years?

Measure the reality of the connection.

Your emotional response should be directly proportionate to the type of connection that you had, if it is an excessively emotional response, you may need to seek professional guidance. If you had a true relationship, for six months or more, you are going to hurt like heck, and of course, the longer the relationship, the more it is going to hurt.

You examined your situation and you find that it was a true relationship of significant length and your significant other is dating someone new.

You know, without a doubt, that the man you were actively loving just a month or two ago is seeing another woman, (*or insert genders as they apply to you*).

It hurts. It makes you sick. It makes you angry.

Who is the first person you are usually angry at for this? Yourself? No, not usually. Your estranged partner? No, you are usually too busy missing them and feeling the pain of their absence. The new person they are seeing? ***Yes***. That's it. Now you've got it.

Our initial reaction to the new person is that they are the evilest, most scheming, most conniving, no-good interloper on the face of the earth. When we call an advisor we ask questions about her like "***Is she after his money***", "***Is she sexually immoral***", "***Is she trying to use him***", etc., etc., etc. We are trying to identify at least one major flaw in the new entity that will reassure us that this new relationship is on shaky ground and that he can't really have feelings for her, he must be with her just for sex, or whatever we convince ourselves it is.

Although sometimes the above conditions may apply, it is infrequent at best. The truth is that usually and customarily our estranged partner finds the new individual to be attractive in some way, feels good around them and wants to get to know them better. It can be a temporary situation, or it can develop into something serious between them, and we frequently ask our metaphysical advisors what it looks like and we answer as honestly as possible.

Sometimes the new relationship looks like it will not bloom. It is a transitional stage that either will lead our lost love back to us, as they realize that their feelings do not develop for the new person, that they still love us. Sometimes the new relationship does look like it will grow and develop. Sometimes the new relationship looks like it is just a transitional thing until our ex is fully our ex and moves on. We look for answers and we hope for the best.

REGARDLESS of what the answers we divine together are, there are several key factors you should focus on to ease your pain and to provide yourself with the best emotional and psychological viewpoint to cope with this situation.

The Dating Game

1) **Energy**. Don't waste your energy trying to make the new person the villain. The new entity may well be unaware of you, may not even know your name and is not out to hurt you specifically. The new person is just living their life and happens to have crossed the path of the same person you care for during a time when an opportunity exists for them to get involved with your ex. (*This does not apply to cheating situations whereby your partner left you to be with them, we are talking about breaks without outside interference*).

2) **Focus.** Remove your focus from your ex (and the new person). Whether or not your readings tell you that your ex is returning, you must set it in your mind that at this point in time **your lover is not yours**, you are two separate people living separate lives. Focus on yourself. Focus on pushing yourself to move forward no matter how difficult.

3) **Break.** Make it a clean break. The **MOST** difficult breakups are those that are not "**clean**". The rubber banding back and forth during an "**unclean break**" is sheer torture emotionally and psychologically. **They call it a break up because it is broken**. Clean breaks mend faster.

4) **Move.** Move on, move forward. Let go. Live your life, don't try to be a voyeur into their life.

5) **Reality.** Live in reality. Don't try to create an illusion for your ex hoping that he is watching. In 99% of cases he is doing all of the above and not focused on you, so don't waste energy sending yourself flowers or trying to make your estranged partner jealous over an imaginary new man in your life, instead, get out there and meet a few new men for real!

The worst case scenario is that he will develop a new relationship and yours will be over for good. In this event, if you have done all that you need to do, you will be well-socialized and already beginning to heal and move on.

The best case scenario is that he will have felt the absence of your energy, found that his feelings for you prevent him from forming a significant new bond with the new person and he returns wanting you back in his life. In this instance, if you have done all of the above, you will be able to make an emotionally intelligent decision about whether or not you even want him back.

If you do take him back, you need to be sure that you are able to put aside any negative feelings that may still remain, or perhaps resurface, when you think of the fact that he was with someone else during your break. This can be difficult and we will discuss this in a future blog.

All Exes Do Not Return.

All Break Ups Are Not Permanent.

Relationship Autopsy

Ok, it's over. It's dead. Done. Fine'. Even your most trusted Advisor has told you this. You've been scouring psychic sites looking for advisors who will tell you that it's not over, but you know in your heart that it is. You've even thought about buying a spell to try to bring him back. It's been a long time since you've heard from him, months and months, and you know through your cyber stalking and the grapevine that he has moved on. You are trying to let go and move on, but you just feel like you can't. Sometimes it feels like you are dying inside. What is your best course of action?

STOP RIGHT THERE.

Promise yourself that when you do call a psychic (if you do), that you will NOT even mention his name. You will not ask about what is going on in his life. You will not ask how he feels about you. You will not ask if he is coming back. You WILL ask how you can begin to heal. You WILL ask what action you can take to begin the process of moving on. You WILL get the support and guidance that you need if you call me, this I promise you. I have been through a difficult breakup myself, I survived, and you will too.

STEP ONE

Perform a Relationship Autopsy.

What was the cause of death here?

Did the heart of the relationship break down due to a lack of maintenance? Did you take each other for granted? Were you mismatched from the beginning? Was the lesson you two were to teach each other completed?

I am one to make lists.

The Dating Game

Fold a paper in two, lengthwise and make two columns. The title of the first column is "Positive", and of course, the title of the second column is "Negative".

Here you will honestly list all of the positives and negatives about the dearly departed relationship.

Which side of your list is longer?

If it is the negative side, why on earth are you so sad? Feel happy that you are now free to start all over again, fall in love all over again, make a fresh start!

If it is the positive side, then yes, you are probably in a lot of pain, and the only way out of the pain is to work through it. You will need to take an inventory at your autopsy.

If this relationship was so positive, you must now decipher how it came to pass away in the manner that it did.

Make another list.

One column is your contribution to the death toll, the other is his.

Again, which side is longer? What do you learn by analyzing your lists? What mistakes have you made that you see a pattern with at this, and other autopsies.

Now that you have ascertained the cause of death, it is time to allow the relationship to rest in peace. Perform your personal memorial service. Put away all of the little reminders and mementoes that keep evoking your sadness. Put them away in a box, somewhere obscure in your house, or if you are really strong, throw them out! Most of us like to hold on to these bittersweet memories, I am a packrat, and I have several boxes like this in storage.

The Dating Game

The healing time for each and every individual varies, a rule of thumb is approximately one month of mourning, (this is a death, isn't it?), for every year of the relationship. Allow yourself time to heal and to feel better. Take some quiet time for yourself. If you have been together for five years, it may well take you five months to start feeling yourself again. Treat yourself to learning something new, beginning to live the life that you have always imagined yourself living, let the travel bug bite you if you are so inclined. Take care of you right now.

If you are suffering physically, not sleeping, not eating, etc., go get a checkup at your family physician. You may unknowingly be suffering from depression and your doctor can help you treat your depression.

Again, take care of you.

If there are belongings of his at your residence, pack them up and ship them to him. Do not hold on to them. They do not represent him. They are either items that are insignificant to him, or he is trying to avoid drama by not picking them up in person. Don't enclose any heartfelt note, and don't damage them, just ship them to him. C.O.D. if he was a cad.

Do not stalk him in any way, shape or form. Don't access his voicemail, don't check his email, and don't go online with his passwords for his match listing or his cell phone. What good is this going to do you? You are staying focused on information that is only going to hurt you. You cannot control him, and it is none of your business what he is up to at this point as he is no longer your partner. Let go. It's called a breakup because it is "broken".

Strictly discipline yourself to putting his life out of your mind and focusing on yours. It is hard, but in awhile, you will begin to feel better, you will be ready to date again and life will resume a normal rhythm for you, but you have to take the time to heal.

When I was divorcing my first husband, my Mother-In-Law imparted these words of wisdom to me, she said, "Brigid, don't be so upset, men are like buses, you stand on a corner long enough, and another one comes by."

Truer words were never spoken.

So when it is over, hard as it may be, accept it, autopsy it, mourn it, grieve it, take time to heal, learn from it, and then move on!

The Dating Game

Music Therapy

I have always been one to take solace in lyrics, that is probably why I enjoy writing poetry so much. I have been a poet since the age of seven, with many poems published over the years, but, unfortunately, I never had any of my poems produced in the form of a song.

Every day, as a Professional Tarot Reader, I speak to clients who are longing for a loved one to return. Along with the tarot reading, if they are interested in listening, I try to encourage them to truly examine their feelings for the person in question to be sure that they, indeed, do want the lover in question to return.

As you may have very well noticed, if you are one of my regular "blog" audience members, I frequently refer to lyrics to express my sentiments and make my points.

So, if you are out there pining for a lost love, please read these lyrics, and if you are like me, the song will play, (*and possibly become stuck*), in your head.

What I want you to do is to truly *"feel"* the song.

Is the person you are missing worthy of all of the grief you are feeling?

When you were together were they kind and caring toward you?

When you were together did they make you feel hurt and anxious on a regular basis?

People do change, but they don't change in significant quantities in a timely manner. True change takes place over extended time and it is intentional and practiced, not just a brief change to get you back for their own purposes with a quick reversal back to old behaviors.

Listen to this song in your head.

The Dating Game

Feel the emotions.

When the song is over, how does the very last line make you feel?

I'll ask that again after your review the lyrics.

Here Come Those Tears Again

(Jackson Browne & Nancy Farnsworth)

Baby here we stand again
Like we've been so many times before
Even though you looked so sure
As I was watching you walking out my door
But you always walk back in like you did today
Acting like you never even went away

Well I don't know if I can
Open up and let you in baby
Here come those tears
Here come those tears again

I can hear you telling me
How you needed to be free
And you had some things to work out alone
Now you're standing here telling me
How you have grown

Here come those tears again
Now you'll tell me how to hold them in
Here come those tears
Here come those tears again

Some other time baby
When I'm strong and feeling fine maybe
When I can look at you without crying

The Dating Game

You might look like a friend of mine
But I don't know if I can
Open up enough to let you in
Here come those tears
Here come those tears again
Just walk away
I'm going back inside and turning out those light
And I'll be in the dark but you'll be out of sight

Okay. Now, how do you feel about the person who has been so heavily on your mind for days, weeks or months?

How does this part **"And I'll be in the dark but you'll be out of sight"**, specifically, make you feel?

Does it make you feel sad? Ok, maybe you still love the lost one and perhaps they were kind to you.

Or does it make you feel empowered? If so, you may very well be on your way to healing and moving past this broken dream.

Look at your estranged lover without the mist in your eyes from your tears. Look at the real person behind the heartache you are feeling.

Were you always the one wanting more and getting less?

Were you always anxious or worried that they would ultimately leave?

What about the happy times, were they truly happy?

Think about it.

Is it time for you to turn out the light?

I Will Survive!

We've all gone through it.

Those terrible break ups when we just don't even feel like getting out of bed in the morning.

Of course, we wonder, if this *"is it"*, if this is a final and permanent break or if there is a light at the end of the tunnel shining on our loved one's return.

Here are some practical tips for surviving this difficult period.

First and foremost, take care of yourself.

You are likely to feel lethargic, disinterested and possibly may be having problems sleeping or sleeping too much.

You may experience an increase or decrease in appetite.

You may find it hard to socialize.

If you are experiencing any of these symptoms to a point where it is disrupting your ability to live your life in a "normal" manner, like missing work, drastic gain or loss in weight, etc., please go to your regular doctor for a physical to determine whether or not you are suffering from a clinical depression. It is possible that this event is a trigger event to throw your brain chemistry off and cause this condition to become active in you and it does require medical treatment.

Second of all, use this time wisely to examine the relationship in question. In my article, ***Relationship Autopsy***, you can find guidelines for performing this mental examination.

The Dating Game

Next, a very difficult step, this is the step that the majority of women who contact me for professional tarot readings and relationship coaching find the most difficult.

You need to move on!

How soon after a breakup should you start to date?

As soon as you can possibly bear it!

Everyone is different on their relationship clock and you may feel hesitant to date others because you are so hoping that your broken relationship will resume. You are afraid that if you go out there and date other men that your estranged partner will give up any notion of returning to you.

This is absolutely not the case!

In fact, it is usually quite the opposite.

When your lost love senses or finds out that you have begun investigating other opportunities he will, (if he has any inclination to do so in the first place), begin his journey back into your life even more quickly than if you put your life on hold waiting to see what happens.

How do I know this?

First of all, I know this for a fact from my own personal life experience.

Second of all, as a **Professional Tarot Reader** and **Relationship Coach**, who has performed over 35,000 professional consultations with clients all over the world, I have seen it literally thousands of times.

Is there a risk that if you move on that he will not return?

Absolutely.

But that risk exists even if you are sitting home by the phone waiting for him to call, or watching his facebook page, or checking to see if he is logged in to Instant Messenger.

Would you rather spend your time apart sitting around using all of your energy building anxiety within yourself trying to determine his moves, or would you rather use that time to be out and about socializing and meeting new people, taking your focus off of your pain, if at least temporarily, and perhaps meet some great people in the process?

The reason that I find most women loathe to begin the moving forward process is that they do not have a realistic perspective on what *"Dating"* actually is.

The majority of women I work with look at Dating as a prelude to a relationship. In fact, there is such a thing as *"Casual Dating"*, which means, hey, you may not think of your Friday night first date as "relationship material", but he is a nice enough guy, within your scale of acceptability for socialization and it beats spending the weekend all alone.

Casual Dating is just that.

You are keeping company for the evening, you already realize that this may not be someone you want to fall in love with or build a relationship with, but his company is pleasant enough to pass the evening, or perhaps even a few evenings with.

There is no pressure as you know that you aren't *"into him"*, so you can relax and just enjoy the dinner or the movie or the show you are attending.

Casual dating also gives you solid practice in the fine art of *"Accepting or Rejecting"* male behaviors.

I cover this in great detail in my article, *"The Dating Game"*.

The Dating Game

When you are not emotionally invested in a male, it gives you a fine playground to practice without feeling that intense anxiety we tend to feel when we are dealing with someone we are in love with. The risk of losing their interest does not come to bear pressure on us as we already are aware that we are not seeing this particular gentleman in the hopes of building a long term relationship, we are "casually dating" for purposes of socialization.

If there is one thing I wish women could grasp and hold, it is that each gentleman we date does **NOT** have to be a black or white, yes or no, Mr. Right or Mr. Wrong. They can actually be somewhere in between, someone to spend time with until the love of our lives return or we meet our next Mr. Right.

When casually dating, it is wise to refrain from sexual intimacy, as **Feminine Energy** women bond through the sex act.

It is also wise to remember that while we are on casual terms, we are not obligated to be monogamous in any way, shape or form with the man in question. We are free to date Tony on Friday, Mark on Saturday, and Joe on Sunday, and perhaps Mark next Friday and Ray next Saturday and Tony next Sunday. It's entirely up to us!

Keep dating casually until one of two things occurs.

1) Our Original Love Interest comes back and commits on the level that we require. (Continue dating casually **UNITL** the commitment you want occurs, **No Exceptions**!) If your primary love interest is Robert, add Robert to your calendar, but don't eliminate Tony, Mark, Joe or Ray until Robert agrees to **YOUR** "Terms of Endearment".

2) In your making the round robin of the dating world, you meet a Joe or Tony or Mark or Ray that you find is an even **BETTER** partner than Robert was. Let's say that Tony turns out to be someone that you dated casually but you are finding him more and more appealing and would really like to be exclusive with him in the hopes of building a new relationship. Keep dating Mark and Joe and Ray until **TONY ASKS** you to

stop seeing other guys and be exclusive with him. Obviously at this point you won't care if Robert returns or not, because you have a fresh, new and optimistic relationship forming with Tony.

Completion of either Steps One or Two means that:

YOU HAVE SURVIVED YOUR BREAKUP!!!

Congratulations!!!!

Chapter Five

Cheating and Affairs

The Dating Game

The Dating Game

Are You Being Lied To?

There are many ways to tell if someone is being dishonest with you. I am going to give you just a few tips that should help you separate out fact from fiction.

Eye Contact

There are two distinct traits used by someone who is trying to deceive you when it comes to maintaining eye contact. One is to avert the eyes away from yours, perhaps they focus on your mouth when they speak rather than your eyes, or they drop their eyes to the left or the right, this is a signal that they are not confident in their ploy and that they may be afraid of discovery. If they are looking up and away to the left or the right they are visualizing their story as they create it.

The second trait is entirely the opposite, they go out of their way to maintain eye contact, the eyes are opened up just a little bit too wide, and they don't blink. This is a tactic used by one who is used to being believed when being deceitful and they are the "more practiced" liars among us. They believe the old adage that people do not look each other in the eye when being deceitful so they go out of their way to maintain the contact, because they are concentrating so hard on keeping the eye contact with you, they forget to blink!

Too Many Details

Everyone has events happen that may delay them or keep them away from time to time, but a classic tactic of the liar is to fill in so many details that you will be astounded by the richness of their story. After all, who would take the time to fabricate the color of the shirt their buddy was wearing and how he had a mustard stain on it???? It's fabricating an alibi..........the more details, the more believable, so why would you double check? Usually these "details" are fragments based on fact, but if you get a six paragraph, detailed explanation of an event, something is up, (or covered up).

Outrageous Stories

Prevaricators tend to hold to the premise that the more outrageous the story, the more likely it is to be true! After all, if a loose alligator in the state of Ohio showed up on their lawn, then traveled around the property snapping phone and power lines with its' mighty jaws, and then coming to rest on the front porch blocking the only exit route, how on earth could they have called you when they said they would? They were trapped in their own home for God's sake!!! Didn't you see it on the local news??

Righteous Silence

OOOOOOH, this one is hard to spot, you must be very careful just in case it is a "righteous silence", typically this is used early on in a relationship before any lies have been "caught". When you question your subject, they take the stance of "I'm not even going to qualify that with a response". Righteous silence lies are very difficult to root out, as, perhaps the subject truly was honest, but if the hints above preceded the righteous silence, well, then, you know that it is an act to manipulate you into believing their story. You usually find out that righteous silence lies were fabricated long after the lie is told because of the high risk of negative confrontation if the subject is actually being truthful. Keep your eyes open for this behavior, if it happens every single time you have an innocent question, the person who is being this self-defensive could well be telling you fibs.

Why do People Cheat?

Let's start with women.

There is a misconception out there that men cheat more frequently than women. In my personal observations, I find this to be untrue. I receive just as many calls from women who are being unfaithful to their husbands and significant others as I do from women who are involved with a man who is either married or seriously involved with another woman.

I do find that when women cheat, they are prone to cheat at a higher percentage due to dissatisfaction with the current primary relationship in hopes that the new lover will provide them with what is missing in that primary relationship. More women than men seem to venture into cheating situations to find their next serious relationship.

Some women, a minority, cheat for the pure excitement and recreational sex, but these are women with very strong masculine energies. They look at the extracurricular relationship as just that, and have no intentions of turning it into a real relationship.

Personally, I believe that it is best (and healthiest), if you are looking for a new relationship, to end the primary relationship before becoming involved with a new lover, and this is simply to avoid the complications and obstacles that the cheating itself brings about.

When a man has a relationship with a woman outside of her marriage or primary relationship a lot of factors go into why he is doing it. Of course, it is possible that he is falling in love and that he wants a relationship with you as much as you do with him, but, again, this is a rarity.

If the "**Other Man**" is single and fully unattached, he may want more with you, he may be one who wants you to end your primary relationship and launch a full-blown relationship with him.

How can you tell?

He will pressure you to leave your partner, he will ask you straight out "**When are you going to end it so we can be together**". It's that simple. He will also be there for you in other ways, perhaps he encourages you to move out of your home or provides financial assistance. If you lover wants to become your number one, you will not have to ask, you will know.

If he is not exhibiting any of the aforementioned behaviors, then he is most likely enjoying the convenience of having a woman in his life without the obligation or commitment a normal relationship would require. If you truly are looking for your next "**real**" relationship, stop wasting your time with this particular guy as he is not going to be there for you when and if you do exit your marriage.

What if your lover is also married? This complicates the situation even more as you are not in a **relationship triangle** you have now entered into a **relationship square**.

Of all the different forms of affairs, this is the most complicated and most likely to fail in transitioning into a dedicated relationship between the two of you.

First of all, you are both cheating. Why are you cheating? You may be looking for an outlet for your sexuality and your personality and want nothing more, if that is the case, you know what you are doing and have no high expectations of the affair changing into something more.

However, if you are looking for more, you may be in danger of being extremely disappointed if he is not also looking to change partners.

In this case, it is very important to find out what his motivations for cheating are and what his expectations from the affair are.

Let's look at why men cheat.

Some men are also looking for their next serious relationship. They are not comfortable leaving the marriage until they have secured a new partner, this is very unhealthy and reeks of *codependency*, however, it does happen.

Some men just succumb to the biological predisposition and their animal instincts. They aren't looking for a new partner, they are looking for pure recreational sex outside of their primary relationship. They may be fun and charming, but their heart lies with their primary relationship, even if their body doesn't.

This may be very hard for some people to comprehend or accept, but a very high risk time for these types of men (*the biologically weak*), is when their wife or life partner is pregnant or has just given birth. Naturally, if you are the other woman you may want to believe that he is cheating on his pregnant wife, or newly maternal girlfriend because he suspects that the child is not his, but in the majority of instances, this is not the case. Sexual experience outside of the primary relationship in this instance is usually due to the male having a *Madonna/Whore* complex, or because the wife or girlfriend is incapable of having sexual relations due to the trauma of having just given birth, or the discomfort of a late-term pregnancy. If the man you are cheating with falls into this category, you are probably having an affair that is purely sexual in nature.

How can you tell if your affair is "just sex"?

The time you spend together is limited to sexual activity. The primary goal being sexual gratification, no dating, no dancing and dining, just hooking up for the physical release and nothing more, is a dead give-away.

Some men cheat because they actually fall in love with another woman.

They didn't plan it. It just happened.

There was something innately missing in their primary relationship and the other woman comes along and possesses the spirit and personality required to evoke feelings of love and attraction within the man that may no longer exist with his wife or significant other.

Sometimes the man does not even realize that his marriage is lacking until he meets this other woman.

How do you know if this is the case with your affair?

Absent the fact that he is married or committed elsewhere, your relationship is caring and passionate. He is attentive to you and your needs, he makes time with you, and he spends time with you doing a lot of things besides the horizontal bop. He will tell you straight out that he is going to leave his marriage and he will tell you when, but the most important thing is that when the time comes ***HE DOES IT***.

Affairs of the heart are complex and complicated, much more so than affairs of the body alone. When the heart is involved, the intensity is there, the sharing is there and the man and the woman are both there.

The Dating Game

It is a myth that all loves that begin while one partner or another or both are committed elsewhere are doomed to failure. There is no blanket formula for love affairs that begin with cheating. If it were true, when some say that "men never marry the woman they cheated with their first wife on", there would be very few second marriages indeed.

I look at it this way. Back in the olden days, when people truly expected to be married for life, people married very young but their life expectancy was much shorter than what it is today.

It is also a fact that as technology provides the human race with more and more leisure time and less time required to focus on utter survival, we have more time to examine relationships, to choose to renew or end or begin again. People grow at different paces.

If two people marry in their late twenties, will those two people grow at the same pace and in the same direction? Sometimes yes, sometimes no, we are not the same person at forty-five that we were at twenty-five or thirty-five, and neither are our spouses and lovers. The person we loved ten years ago may have evolved (*or failed to evolve*) into someone we no longer want for a life mate, and so we move on.

Of course, it is always best to begin a relationship one-on-one, but there are times when this just doesn't happen. We can't judge a book by its' cover, nor can we project that a relationship is doomed to failure because of a less-than-perfect beginning. In the same vein, we can't project that a relationship will last because of love and passion, that goes for first marriages and relationships just as much as it does for subsequent ones.

Why do people cheat?

The list is endless. This is just the tip of the iceberg and the most frequent causes that I have seen in my personal and professional experience. Sometimes it's pure selfishness or boredom, sometimes it is looking for love.

I have seen many hearts broken through these types of love affairs, but I have also seen multiple cases of joy, happiness and success. There is no magic formula for success, but neither is there an automatic failure due to circumstance, each case needs to be reviewed independently of any other. If you are in this situation, believe me, you are **NOT** alone.

The Dating Game

Are You The "Other Woman"?

There are two sides to every story, and sometimes there may actually be three or four.

When we involve ourselves in an affair with someone who is already committed elsewhere, *i.e. has a steady girlfriend (or boyfriend), lives with someone, or is married,* we are involving ourselves in an emotionally risky business.

Someone is going to be hurt.

That's a cold hard fact.

It is the rare situation indeed where one partner is cheating and either the original partner or the outside partner does not get hurt.

I have written many blogs on the subject of **Why People Cheat** and the reasons are as varied as there are grains of salt in the ocean, the cold hard facts are, it happens. Many times it happens when we least expect it.

Do people go out and think, *"Gee, I'm going to go out tonight and find myself a married person to fall in love with?"* No. Attraction, destiny, life circumstances, soul connections, physical desire, dissatisfaction, they are all ingredients in the recipe for an affair.

If you are the *"Other Woman"*, (or man), in a *Relationship Triangle*, this blog is being written for you to try to help you gain some insight into your situation. *If you are an injured party in an adulterous affair, please bypass this blog, as it may anger or upset you and you really should read no further.* I will have written blogs, such as, **Surviving an Affair** to help you address the aftermaths of an affair. *(Yes, I have been cheated on before, but I try to look at things from all angles, so please, I am not condoning affairs, just analyzing and working with them for my clients who are experiencing this side of the mountain right now.)*

The Dating Game

First of all, you need to know what the limitations of your current situation are. Yes, someday he may leave his wife, but you can't live in the future, you live in the **NOW**, so you must focus on the now. If he is not married, but living with a woman, (*or man*), it is nearly as complicated as if he were married, so this will apply to you as well. If he is not yet engaged and it is just a girlfriend/boyfriend situation, there is no reason for him not to be out of the other relationship already. You need to know if it is not a serious commitment to the other partner at this time, and he (or she) is seeing both of you, your lover is unlikely to end that other relationship to be solely with you.

If he is married and seeing you, you need to realize that your plans are always going to be subject to last minute changes. Last minute cancellations are just as prominent as last minute get-togethers.

You will also be spending most, if not all, major holidays alone, while he is enjoying the company of his family, including his spouse.

You will not be able to openly share your relationship with the public, discretion will be a necessity, and so therefore, you will never get to know his parents, siblings, his children or his circle of friends. *(Unless he does divorce in the future).*

You will be living in the shadows.

The married man who is dating another woman may be a man who never has any intention of leaving his marriage, or he could be ready to leave and for any one of a thousand reasons, the timing may not yet be right for him.

The question you must ask yourself is, what kind of a relationship do you really want?

Do you want to suffer through the uncertainty, possibly years, of wondering if he is ever going to get divorced? Has he ever even mentioned the **"D"** word to you?

The Dating Game

Do you want a man that can take you out in public and share 100% of his life with you, or are you satisfied with 50% or less?

Are you prepared for the backlash that is likely to occur if your affair is ever discovered by his wife and children? It is not likely to be pleasant.

If your bond to him is so strong that you feel that you are ready and willing to deal with this uncomfortable situation, then here are some ways to cope.

Always be aware that no matter how firmly he promises to follow through on any plans that he makes with you, that *"The Wife"* card will always trump you. Always remind yourself as you anticipate a weekend getaway that yes, it can be postponed, yet again. If you keep your expectations low, you will not be devastated at last minute cancellations.

Try not to be ready to see him at the drop of a hat. He will find himself unexpectedly free and available at times, and will contact you wanting to see you desperately as he has some unexpected free time. You will be very tempted to take advantage of each and every opportunity to see him, but if you are wise, you will not allow this to occur as it teaches him that he is your priority, though you are not his.

Remember, he is romancing you against your better judgment, so these types of affairs can be extremely romantic and dramatic, grand gestures and excessive professions of love are not unusual, he has to convince you that although he is committed elsewhere he is worth your time. Take everything he says with a grain of salt. *Married men who have girlfriends lie. This is a cold hard fact.* If he did not lie, he would not be dating you and he would not be cheating on his wife. If he is lying to his wife, don't think for a second that he isn't lying to you.

One of the biggest lies that married men who cheat tell, is that they don't sleep with their wives anymore, many of them will even claim to have separate bedrooms, don't believe it, they all say that. If he is still married to her he is still sleeping with her and yes, they are still having sex. With that in mind, the biggest mistake *"the other woman"* makes is being exclusive to the married man she is dating. Until he files for a divorce, you should continue dating other single and available men. It is best if you can walk away from the married guy and say *"look me up after your divorce"*, but if you simply can't, please continue to date men that are available concurrently, otherwise you will be very lonely at times.

Be careful who you share information about your affair with. People love to gossip, and a secret is only a secret when only one person knows about it. Even some of your best friends may judge you harshly for dating a married man, so be very careful about who you discuss it with.

Set a time limit for your affair.

Unless you want to be like Katherine Hepburn and spend decades as the other woman, only to have him die married to his wife, bring up the discussion of divorce early on. If he does not give you a timeframe, walk away. If he says he is waiting for the kids to finish high school, seriously consider their current ages, if they are still very young, walk away. If he set a timeframe and it has passed without him going into the process of divorce, walk away.

In all of this, you must consider as well, how he speaks of his current wife.

Does he refer to her respectfully and honestly state the reasons for his dissatisfaction with his marriage? If that is the case, he respects women and probably just outgrew the relationship.

Does he run her down and call her names and degrade her? Well, in that case, it may make you temporarily feel good because it convinces you he's not in love with her, but, remember, that someday you may be in her shoes and would you like him to talk about you like that? It's disrespectful. Never trust someone that has nothing but bad things to say about their partner or their exes because someday they could be speaking of you that way.

It is a high risk situation that you are in. You could very easily have your heart broken. He may stay married forever. It does happen. You can possibly spend years on the fringes of his life loving him and hoping for change only to be disappointed in the end. It is best to avoid the situation all together if possible, but if it happens to you, you are not alone and if you need help surviving it and coping with it and trying to make your decisions you may need to seek outside counsel to discuss your situation.

Cheating and Affairs

I think that it is very important to cover this topic in my blog so as to give you some perspective on the dynamics of these difficult situations. I am very nonjudgmental, and in my practice I work with people on all sides of this issue. Please do not read any further if you are stringently offended by this subject matter.

There are many different types of affairs to consider. We have the situation where a single woman gets involved with the married man, the reverse of the same by gender, two married people becoming involved with each other outside of their marriage, and the brief encounter type of affair that is more like a fling, to name just a few.

Let's examine the affair where a single woman starts to date a married man, knowingly. This scenario will not apply to any of the other "types" of affairs, but there is some cross-over to the other types.

We will focus on the involvement of a woman with a married man with full knowledge of his marital status, this will not apply to those cases where he misrepresents his marital status.

This situation is much more prevalent than most people think. A lot of people still think in the archaic mindset of the secret "mistress" being kept by the married man. This is extremely rare. Most "other women" are extremely self-sufficient and many times they are actually helping the married man meet his obligations in some way.

So, how does this all begin?

People fall in and out of love all of the time. Affairs of this nature can spring up when a marriage begins to turn stale or cold. Many times affairs like this can pop up without the wife ever even realizing that there is a problem. Sometimes we just can't control who we fall in love with, or when. Of course there are the types of affairs where men cheat purely for sexual gratification, those types of affairs are rampant, but they are usually the fling type of affair and not the type where the married man builds an actual relationship with the single woman.

Let's talk about the extramarital affair that occurs due to a pure attraction physically and emotionally to someone other than the original spouse. Frequently, when we are not having our needs met, we will seek to have those needs met wherever we can. The business of marriage is not the "happy ever after" story that many of us fantasized about during our youths, but a partnership in dealing with the business of living. Paying bills, raising children, shopping, housekeeping, financial planning, buying homes and other assets, this is what marriage truly boils down to. You do all of these things together, you share each other sexually and emotionally and perform the duties and tasks required to live from day to day, together. We sometimes can go on for years in a marriage, practicing the business of living, and someday, somehow, we manage to meet "someone else" and something within changes.

In the scenario I am presenting, there may be no major issues between the spouses to act as a catalyst for change, but in meeting this new person, sometimes a married man will feel that "old feeling" of falling in love again, and even though the marriage itself may appear stable, the foundation begins to crack.

Some men are of such high moral standards that they will never cheat, no matter what.

Some men hit a situation like this and are tempted, but do not go beyond the level of flirtation.

Some men hit a situation like this and do decide to pursue an affair, but they know that they will never divorce, they will just continue on with the marriage and the day to day business of it, and build a relationship concurrently with another woman. This is the ultimate in self gratification and honestly, it is the primary scenario that occurs. They do not want any disruption to the pitter patter of their daily lives with their wives and families, but they also want the gratification of the birth of the new relationship outside of the marriage. They may very well fall in love with the other woman, but, they will always find a reason not to leave the wife. This is a very dangerous situation for a single woman to be in if she truly wants a full-blown relationship with the man in question.

Time and time again these women will be let down, put on hold, asked to wait, or told point blank that the man is never going to leave by the man himself.

Then we have the final scenario.

This is the rarest of the extra-marital affair situations.

In this situation the married man actually does fall completely in love with the other woman and he does leave his wife. It does happen, although it is not the norm. I know of at least seven cases where the man in question did divorce and successfully move into the new relationship with the other woman, however, I know of no less than one hundred cases where the man never left the wife and continued to live a double life. I know this through personal experience and knowledge and also through my practice as an Advisor and Relationship Coach.

This last case is what most women who find themselves in this precarious position are hoping for, but honestly, it does not happen very often for a variety of reasons.

There are several things that you need to know if you allow yourself to take the risk of becoming involved with a married man on a relationship level.

Know that he will never be able to be brutally honest with you while he is still married. How can he be honest, he has to lie and steal time BOTH ways. He's not going to give you the full story on his home life. The marriage may not even be difficult, it could just be "lackluster" and that could be why he is cheating. Odds are the married man is getting along with his wife much better than how he presents it to you. It is extremely rare for a married man to tell you that his relationship with his wife is amicable, so he will exaggerate any problems that may or may not exist.

Know that on his list of priorities that you will always be second behind his wife and if he has children, you will drop down to at least a priority three. This means that you will be dealing with a lot of cancellations, broken promises, missed calls and postponed events during this relationship. You will experience more last minute cancellations and postponements in a relationship like this than in any other type of relationship. If his wife decides, on the morning of the day that you two promised to spend together, perhaps even a special occasion like your birthday, that she needs him to go with her to the shopping outlets two hours out of town, he will be going shopping and you will be waiting at home alone. If he can't break free to call you out of her earshot, you will be sitting by a silent phone wondering what happened.

In 90% of cases like this, discretion is a must. There are cases where the man may not care if he gets caught or not, or he may be somewhat of a risk taker for being found out, but these are rare.

No one likes to be cheated on, so even if he truly does intend to get a divorce at some future time, he is not going to willingly allow his future ex to build an arsenal of weaponry against him.

This means that your public time together will be limited at best, some couples in this situation do not socialize at all for fear of discovery, many travel out of town to see each other, etc. Don't expect to be able to do the "normal" things like going to a popular restaurant in your locality where you might bump into mutual acquaintances etc., be prepared to accept a very clandestine social life together. Some people find this exciting and romantic, but usually the women get to a point where they do want some normalcy after a time. This may never happen for you.

Expect to spend all major holidays alone. You will have to schedule your New Year your Christmas etc. on days that aren't actually the holiday as it is very rare for the married man to be able to make contact at these times. It makes for a lonely existence.

The most frequently told lies by married men are that they no longer have sex with their wives and that they do not sleep in the same room in the house as their wives, perhaps they say they have a separate bedroom or that they sleep on the couch. This is utter nonsense. If they are still married, they are having sex, it may be perfunctory sex and it may not be frequent, but they are still having sex. As far as sleeping arrangements go, that's a lot of baloney as well, if they are still married, in the same home, they are sharing that bed in the master bedroom.

The most frequently used excuses for not getting a divorce, even though they love you, are that they are concerned about their finances, they are waiting for the kids to graduate high school, they are waiting for the kids to finish college, they are waiting until after their daughter gets married, has a baby, their son launches his law practice, etc. etc. etc. The list is never ending because there is always a future responsibility or concern within a family, and his wife is part of that family.

If a man wants a divorce, he will get one. It will not matter how old his children are, how far along they are in their pregnancies or law practices, he will file.

Does the married man love you? If this has been going on for some time and the time you spend together consists of more than just sexual experiences, then it is possible that he does.

Will he leave his wife? In the majority of cases, the answer is no.

If you are entering into or already in a situation like this, you have two choices, either accept it as is and realize the down side of the situation or tell him you are ending it if he doesn't get a divorce, and end it until he does. Those are the choices. That's it. You don't wait, you don't give him time. And while he is married you should definitely not be exclusive to him, you should continue to date other people, preferably single, until he can be exclusive to you. Period.

And remember this, while he has the support and companionship of his wife as he goes about paying his mortgage and his light bill and buying a new car and feeding the cat and walking the dog, YOU are alone, and must handle the mundane matters of life ALONE. This is a very difficult way to live, and usually you can't just pick up a phone and call the married man in question, you have to communicate on some sort of "schedule". If you can avoid this situation, please do so. If you are already emotionally bonded into one, you are living in a high stress situation and you actually may benefit by seeking outside counsel to discuss your situation and your particular issues.

What if he does leave his wife?

We'll talk about that in another blog.

How Virtual Affairs Can Be Just As Damaging As Real Life Affairs

Unfortunately, the pain that a partner feels when they discover that their loved one is carrying on a virtual affair is every bit as hurtful as that of a physical affair in the real world.

Regardless of whether the "*affair*" is heavy flirting or clandestine contact with a person on the other side of the world, the feelings of trust and betrayal are just as intense to the injured party.

Although a cyber affair can be chalked up to the realm of "*fantasy*", there is another live human being on that other keyboard communicating with the wayward partner and that poses as big a risk as hooking up with a coworker at lunch time.

Many may feel that virtual flings cause an overreaction in their loved one when they are caught due to the misperception that it is just a "*fantasy*". In today's electronic age of email, cell phones, chat rooms and text messaging, the virtual affair can create a bond that exists outside of cyberspace and is occurring right in your living room under your partner's nose. This is not a fantasy, this has invaded your very living space and it is real.

This is a betrayal of trust in just as devastating of a way as any "*real life*" affair.

Communication is a form of intimacy. Sharing thoughts and feelings with your virtual liaison' is just as unfaithful as pillow talk with a physical lover.

When one finds themselves engaging in this cyber flirtation, one must ask themselves, why? Why do I find it so intriguing to engage in electronic communication with this unknown entity when the partner I portend to love is right in the next room watching television? Something is lacking in the union and one's energy would be better spent logging out and going into the living room and having a heart to heart talk with their partner to resolve whatever issues are causing you to be tempted to stray, even if it is "*only*" in cyberspace.

When one finds themselves the injured party, or "***cheated on***", virtual reality takes on just as much form and structure as the room they are standing in and the emotional response is going to be just as painful as if you caught your partner in bed with another.

Trust has been broken, and with today's electronic communication systems it is very difficult to repair. A partner who discovers the virtual affair will be hard pressed to trust the cheating partner to log on, have a cell phone, use their email at work, without the constant doubt, thinking, "***is the communication still going on?***".

Rather than allowing a simple, quick, virtual flirtation to escalate into something that can do irreparable damage to your primary relationship, talk to your loved one about what is missing in your real life relationship and do some preventative maintenance before you find yourself alone with only your cyber love to keep you company. A keyboard can't keep you warm at night, your real life partner can.

The Dating Game

Once a Cheater, Always a Cheater?

My answer to this statement is no.

There are far too many reasons why people cheat to begin with to be able to cover it with a blanket statement like this.

In my professional practice as a **Relationship Coach**, I speak to literally thousands of people on all sides of this relationship dilemma.

I find that the primary reason for women to cheat is that they are "**piggy-backing**" their relationships. Frequently they are caught up in a codependent cycle and cheat on their primary relationship in the pursuit of a new partner.

Once a new partner has been successfully attained, these women typically return to monogamous behavior, and as long as the current relationship remains satisfying, they remain faithful.

When men cheat, they are more frequently doing so for sexual gratification, and although there are many men who enjoy and pursue relationships that are explicitly sexual outside of their primary relationship, I also find men that actually do fall in love with the other woman.

At times, they are unable to leave the primary relationship due to familial obligations and maintain concurrent relationships, thus prolonging a state of infidelity, however, there are men who want to follow their hearts' desire and leave their primary relationship to begin a new primary relationship with the other partner.

Because a relationship starts while one, (or both), partners are being unfaithful to someone does not automatically preclude them to repeating the pattern.

It also holds true that if someone has cheated on you in the past, they are not necessarily going to continue to cheat moving forward, as long as the core issue that initially caused the cheating is resolved.

If a former cheater is happy and satisfied it is highly unlikely that they will wander again.

What prevents a cheater from cheating again is understanding the root cause of why the cheating occurred in the first place. Yes, there are habitual cheaters, but these are the minority not the majority.

The majority of "*cheaters*" do so because there is a dissatisfaction in their current relationship, remove that dissatisfaction and you no longer have a cheater.

He Left His Wife, Now What?

Ok, you had been in the midst of a fairly serious affair with this married man. You survived all of the mayhem as discussed in my blog ***Cheating and Affairs*** and now you think you're troubles are over.

Stop.

This is not the end of your problems, it is just a new set of challenges.

There are two ways that this situation can go. Let's explore both of them.

Scenario One

The married man you love has left his wife and your relationship is still "iffy".

Scenario Two

The married man you love has left his wife and he is making definitive plans for a future with you.

In **Scenario One** you may be dealing with a man who has spent years in an unwanted marriage. Although the time you had together may have had it's good points, and you may have thought that he loved you, he may feel that he has been living his life in a very restrictive manner and the divorce now gives him the freedom to live as truly single again.

Your relationship with him may start to suffer. He may blame you for his divorce, pick fights for no reason, cheat on you, or outright leave you.

Some men, when they divorce, get a feeling of "***out of the frying pan and into the fire***" and they will never commit to the woman that they were with when they left their marriage. This happens in about 50% of the cases I have worked with when the man does exit his marital commitment.

Many times the catalyst to the breakup of the affair in question is the pressure that the woman who has been waiting for years applies to the man to progress the relationship.

The woman may feel that she has spent more than enough time waiting for this to be real, and now that he is "*free*", he should immediately commit to her. The man in question, as stated, may need a period of time to spread his wings, sow his wild oats again, and you, the woman in waiting, may find that not only is your waiting not over, but the relationship itself may be falling to pieces just when you thought your dreams were coming true.

In some cases, this stage, or breakup, may only be temporary, however, more often than not, this is when the affair loses its' appeal and things start riding the highway to hell.

Scenario Two

Your married man left his wife with the explicit intention of building a life with you, and he has made that very clear to you.

Good for you.

Now, perhaps, you believe that you can really start your relationship for real and that you can have a fresh start.

Although this scenario, rare as it is, can initially be a very happy one for the two of you as a couple, you're not out of the woods yet.

First of all, there may well be a very difficult (*and expensive*) divorce proceeding for your married man to contend with. Child custody battles, drawn out settlement negotiations are common.

Divorces of this type are usually much more vindictive than any other type of divorce because of the involvement of the third party (**you**), no one likes to be cheated on, and your married man's soon to be ex may be trying to hurt him in any way(s) she can to punish him for cheating.

Even worse, the soon-to-be ex-wife is even more hurt and angry because if she is aware that he intends to build a future with you, he has moved on very quickly and that stings. No one likes to be replaced, especially before they are "**gone**". So be prepared for a nasty divorce battle.

Now, there is his family to contend with. Do you actually believe that his children and his parents are going to welcome you with open arms? To be realistic, the children may very well hate you for the rest of their lives for disrupting their home life. Even if it wasn't happy, and the parents were fighting a lot, it was the "norm" and their dad was a part of their day-to-day living, and now you "**took him away**". They are likely to resent you big time. If the ex-wife is particularly vindictive, she will poison the children in many ways against you and probably against him too. This does not make for a happy foundation for a blended family.

Finances may be difficult for a long time to come when the divorce is over. He will likely have child support and possibly alimony as well, so you will have to continue to contribute to the financial stability of your pairing, more so than if this situation did not exist.

Be aware that you may begin to resent the additional financial burdens that the ex-wife and children present, the younger the children, the longer you are restricted.

He may still be required to live a separate life when it comes to his children. To keep peace he may have to keep his relationship with his children separate from you, it happens very often, so keep your fantasies of a happy blended family to a minimum.

His parents may or may not accept you, it will depend upon your individual circumstances, so again, you may feel like you are still an outsider.

You will also need to be concerned about joint assets. Suppose he moves into the home you already own and you marry. Be sure you have a will defining how your assets will be distributed. What if you have children as well, if you die first and do not define who the house goes to in your will, your now-husband will inherit it automatically, and then when he passes on who gets it? Your kids? His kids? You must look at the situation realistically to protect yourself as well as any children you have on your own.

As time goes on, the situation may improve, children grow up, exes move on, people adapt, but be aware that these are just a few of the challenges you may face when you enter into this volatile situation. People fall in and out of love all of the time.

Your situation is not unusual to say the least, but it is more challenging in the obstacles and pressures that come your way due to the way that it began.

Keep that in mind and prepare yourself emotionally and psychologically.

The Dating Game

Chapter Six

Modern Day Issues

The Dating Game

I AM NOT YOUR SCRUBBING BUBBLE!

Remember those old bathroom foam cleaning commercials with the little scrubbing bubbles calling out *"We work hard so you don't have toooooooo......"* as they spun down the drain?

Think about them the next time a person in your life, be it an adult son or daughter, sister, brother, lover or husband tries to force you into the role of *"enabler"* in their life. Just conjure up that image in your mind, think of yourself being sucked down the drain of codependency, and say *"NO"*.

They might be asking you to add them to your cell phone plan. Maybe they want you to lend them money or clean their apartment for them. Perhaps they ask you to let them use your car or buy them groceries. Maybe they ask you to forgive them for not holding to their word for the umpteenth time, or any one of the thousands of manipulative forms of assistance they seek when they are just too dysfunctional to behave like responsible adults.

Codependent relationships are not limited to substance abusers and their kin, they are real and alive in every relationship dynamic out there. There is *absolutely nothing* wrong with helping your loved ones, *nothing at all*, the question is, *is your loved one doing the work required to help themselves?*

Are they just a little short on cash, or have they been unemployed for a lengthy period of time, or unable to manage their cash flow or hold a job? Everyone comes up short on occasion, especially in the current economy, but some of us are scrubbing bubbles and some of us are not.

If you are working diligently every day and use your resources wisely, why should you take your hard earned cash and hand it over to the adult child who has not been gainfully employed in six months?

When you saved regularly when times were good and paid all your bills on time and your significant other played and partied and scattered his funds to the wind without setting up a reserve, why should you add him to your cell phone plan when his is shut off and increase your monthly debt?

When your husband golfed all summer and bought himself new clubs, a new bag, nice equipment and turned down overtime to do so and finds himself short on the car payment, should you take money out of your pocket and make up the difference?

Absolutely not!

Taking care of yourself and your own responsibilities and ensuring that your resources are allotted as you budget is ***not selfish***, it's ***wise and healthy***.

Will your loved one have problems because you don't help them out? Probably, but if they are an adult, they need to solve their problems for themselves, you are not their ***"rescuer"***.

It is ***not your job to make them happy!*** That is a job that every man (and woman) must do for themselves!

Stop being an enabler! Will you lose the love of your significant other if you do not let him borrow your car and use up all of your gas to run errands? ***NO!*** If you do, you never had it!

Remember, ***"I am NOT your Scrubbing Bubble!"***

You work hard so that you can enrich your own life, you don't work hard so that your adult child, lover, husband or friend ***DOESN'T*** have to!

Please do not make the mistake of thinking that providing your loved one with their own private ***"bail out"*** is going to make them grateful, thankful or respectful. ***Quite the opposite is true.***

The Dating Game

When a normal healthy adult knows that they can come to you and just dump all of their troubles on your doorstep and you start *"scrubbing them away",* when they should be cleaning up their own mess, the only thing that is going to happen is you will find yourself endlessly scrubbing that doorstep. More and more and more problems will find their way onto your stoop.

The loved one now knows that he or she can manipulate you. Your adult daughter can't afford daycare? Grandma will either babysit or pay for it. Think about it. If she has the money for a weekly manicure at the beauty salon, why should you pay for her daycare expenses?

The boyfriend who has lost yet another job and still can't pay his half of the rent, happily takes a few weeks off to *"chill"* before launching his next job search. He is perfectly comfortable sleeping until noon and playing video games and surfing facebook all day while you are up at six to leave for your full time job that you've had for four years? He never seems to quite *"catch up"* with his half of the expenses. Why? Because **YOU WORK HARD SO HE DOESN'T HAVE TO!** Is that why you are working so hard? I think not.

Hold your adult loved ones to the same standard that you hold yourself. No exceptions, no excuses and *you will find yourself having happier and healthier adult-to-adult relationships.*

Should Women Feel Trapped in a Marriage that Just Doesn't Work?

In an age when we have a firm legal system in place to ensure the protection of children and divorced spouses and the continuance of financial support, there is no reason on earth that anyone, male or female, should feel trapped in a dysfunctional marriage. We all deserve to be happy and contented in our lives. When a marriage becomes too difficult to tolerate, separation and divorce can allow us to start anew and seek happiness again.

Some of the top reasons that women in particular may feel trapped in a troubled marriage are religious obligations, financial (lifestyle) concerns, children and fear of being alone.

Perhaps we should address these top concerns individually.

Religious obligations vary based upon faith and denomination, however, discussing your concerns with your religious leader can help you to determine if leaving the marriage is right for you. Are the difficulties in your marriage irreconcilable? If so, any professional clergy will be able to advise you as to how the termination of the marriage will affect your standing in your religion. If you religion is extremely orthodox and does not allow divorced members to continue to worship, you may have to choose a new spiritual outlet that is more forgiving of human error. A religion has no authority to dictate that you must remain married if you are so extremely unhappy that you feel trapped.

Many women in the past felt trapped in dysfunctional marriages due to financial dependency. That is not the case today, at least not in the United States. Our family courts and domestic relation sections ensure that spousal support and child support requirements are enforced. Most modern women are perfectly capable of supporting themselves and their children if necessary and should be able to maintain the same lifestyle for themselves and the children when combining their earnings with support received from the estranged spouse. The bottom line is, is maintaining a material lifestyle worth enduring the marriage continuing? The assumption here is that the marriage is causing extreme discomfort and unhappiness. There is no reason to feel trapped, you can leave if you are unhappy and your spouse will be obligated to contribute to your support and the support of any children you may have.

Staying together for the sake of the children is an argument for maintaining a difficult marriage since life began. At the core of this argument are two key factors, one is maintaining a standard of living that the children are accustomed to, this is addressed above concerning financial dependency. The second key factor is maintaining relationships with both parents, having a father and a mother actively involved in the children's upbringing. Again, we must cite the court systems of today which, even in the most difficult of divorce proceedings, will regulate visitation schedules and custody issues. Unless a parent is unfit, there is no reason why they cannot continue to have a healthy and productive relationship with their children. Children being raised in an unhappy and stressful household will fare much better if they are in a happy home, regardless of whether there are two parent figures or one on premises. Psychologically it is more important for children to see a positive resolution to conflict rather than continued endurance of an unhappy and unhealthy marriage. Teaching your children how to be happy is much more productive than teaching your children how to submit to stress and practice conformity to societal standards.

A fear of being alone once one has exited their marriage can keep some women in a difficult marriage much longer than is healthy or necessary. Starting over after divorce is a major life stressor and can keep a woman frozen in time, unable to act, out of shear fear of the unknown. Many social outlets today can help a newly divorcing woman to transition into being single again. Singles clubs run by churches and social organizations, volunteer work, returning to the work force, all of these events will widen the woman's social circle and allow opportunity to build a new support network. The recently divorced woman may be quite surprised to find that isolating within a bad marriage had her feeling much more alone than she is post divorce when she has the freedom to socialize and interact at will.

Should women feel trapped into staying in marriages that do not work? Absolutely not. The only one who can trap a woman into remaining in a bad marriage is the woman herself. Freedom is just one decision away.

The Dating Game

Are Modern Day Relationships Giving Men Excuses To Escape Responsibility?

Modern day relationships are not only giving men excuses to escape from responsibilities, *they are making them run from responsible relationships!*

Not only has the last forty years of child rearing produced multi-generations of women who can *"bring home the bacon, fry it up in a pan"*, but they have also allowed men to feel that women should be *"equal"* partners in relationships. Nothing wrong with equality, but when the scales of relationships were set so off-kilter to begin with, society has thrown the scale to the extreme opposite.

True role reversals in modern relationships are a rarity.

Women of my generation and those in succeeding generations are and have been groomed for success in career and education first and foremost, this was not the norm historically, historically men received this grooming while young women were groomed to be nurturers and providers of safe havens and beautiful homes.

Now, we women want it all *and we go after it all.*

Our feminine energies have given way to strong and assertive masculine energies which serve us well in school and on the job but undermine our ability to allow men to feel an equal responsibility in the relationship arena.

Women are now expected to earn good incomes, own great cars and homes and toys and trinkets and still provide primary household maintenance and primary child care, while men are still groomed for the most part in the *"same old way"* but without benefit of developing their nurturing side to bring the relationship scales into balance.

Men want to be coddled and cared for by the modern woman just as they did fifty years ago by our grandmothers. We are surely on our way to creating a gender androgyny that is likely to continue unless we learn to bring the yin and yang back into balance.

When a man marries today, he assumes that not only will his wife contribute economically to the marriage, typically she earns just as much if not more than he does, but he also assumes that she will take care of the home and the children. He assumes that his primary obligation is to continue to provide half of the economic security of the union. Should the marriage fail, he feels he is doing *"his fair share"* by providing child support, but typically, the weekly checks and a weekly or biweekly visit are as far as his connection with the family he helped create will go. The male will then begin to move on, unencumbered, to his next modern woman while the original wife and mother now assumes *100% of the parenting responsibilities.*

The electronic age of dating is not helping this problem.

We have multiple social websites available at the touch of a button. Communication is immediate through cell phone, text or email. Anywhere and at anytime men and women of today can communicate with each other. This not only creates a lack of a sense of *"urgency"* to communicate in relationships, but it also makes it extremely easy to fall prey to temptations outside of the primary relationship. A cyber flirtation may seem innocuous, but sooner or later these cyber relationships come out of the computer and into your living room.

Insecurities in modern relationships create fertile ground for infidelity and relationship *"jumping"*.

A woman feels safe and secure if her man is texting her through the day, that communication being constant, the man may grow bored and easily find another female to communicate with. At first it may be innocent, but when the primary relationship begins to feel to bear the weight of responsibility, *"poof"*, frequently the man moves on to a weightless and seemingly responsibility free relationship.

The Dating Game

Men can now look at women as capable and strong entities, capable of providing for themselves and others, women can do it all. When he no longer is *"having fun"* or enjoying the relationship it is just too easy for him to move on and find a new fresh start, leaving the woman behind to be the responsible one and the male feeling no sense of guilt, because, hey, *"She can take care of herself"*.

What Do Your Children Really Need to Know About Your Divorce?

Children are resilient and as parents we tend to forget that they are and try to protect them from anything which will cause them pain and discomfort.

When a set of parents decide to divorce, it is important that they can at least agree on how they are going to communicate this to the children that they share. Divorce of one's parent has the potential to become life-long psychological baggage if not handled in a nurturing and compassionate fashion.

The circumstances surrounding the cause of the divorce will play a key factor in exactly how and what is shared with the offspring involved.

If the divorce is due to basic incompatibility and there are no extenuating factors such as abuse involved, the children can be told what to expect in a straightforward manner. The age of the children is the second factor to be considered. The younger the child, the more simple the explanation and foundation for expectations should be.

In the event that the situation is more complicated, that there is spousal abuse, an extremely upsetting extramarital affair, substance abuse, abandonment or some other serious factor, the parents should be sure to use age appropriate filtering of information. In these cases, it is most likely that only one parent will be doing the communicating with the children and care should be taken to allow the children to maintain a reasonable level of respect for the erring parent. A laundry list of the absent parent's faults and misdeeds will only harm your children, if the absent parent is not going to see the children on a regular basis after the divorce, the children do need to be advised of that fact. For a young child it can be expressed as "you are probably not going to see mommy/daddy for a very long time, but I will be here for you". If the child is old enough to understand that a volatile situation has come to an end, a simple and honest statement of "I do not know when you will see mommy/daddy again" will suffice.

The focus should be on what the children can expect in the future as far as the availability of the absent parent and how their lives will be directly, and indirectly, affected in an honest and realistic manner. Instilling false hopes in a child of any age can be shattering to the psyche.

When you are informing your children that you are divorcing the most important element of the information you share is that you lay a very firm and realistic foundation for the expectations that the children will have post divorce. If you are not the parent who will be in majority custody you need to be absolutely certain that you will be able to live up to any visitation schedule that you plant in your children's thoughts.

Children of all ages tend to trust their parents implicitly. Do not sugar coat the future for them. Be realistic in your description of the future, painful though it may be, it will save the children much pain in the future if you exceed or meet their expectations rather than fall short of them.

Your children do not need to know why you are divorcing, a simple statement that the marriage has ended but that you will both still be their parents is enough.

Answer their questions as honestly as possible and begin to familiarize them with how their schedules will be affected.

If you are going to have a visitation schedule with your children inform them of that schedule, and by all means, stick to it. Try to keep as much stability in your parental relationships with your children as is possible and share with them the fact that you will still continue to be present in their lives for those routine activities you usually and customarily attend to.

If you are the custodial parent, inform them of any changes in residence or schools they can expect and reassure them that you love them and will still be there for them.

If you are the parent who is exiting the home, tell your children where you will be living. Take your children to your new residence and show them around, show them what space will be theirs, assure them that they are going to have a second home where they can spend time with you.

If you are moving some distance away and your visitation schedule will be less frequent you should take advantage of today's technology such as web cams and video conferencing to spend time with them on a regular basis. Invest in the equipment and spend time teaching them how to utilize it. Inform your children of how to contact you even if you have to buy them their own cell phones to do so. Your children need to know that they can reach out to you whenever they need to.

The responsibility is yours, you are the adults. Although anger and resentment can well be boiling between you and your soon-to-be ex spouse, you must make every effort to lay a solid foundation of realistic expectations and communication lines between the children and each parent.

Remember that, although you are likely to be in emotional turmoil at this juncture, you need to instill a sense of security and safety in your children to protect their emotional and psychological health.

The Dating Game

When is it Appropriate to Introduce Your Date to Your Children?

Many people are in such a hurry to progress their new relationships that they prematurely introduce what later become "casual dating experiences" to their children.

So, when is it appropriate to introduce your date to your kids?

When we find ourselves in the role of a single parent it is inevitable that at some point we are going to want to enter the social arena of dating again.

The wise parent will refrain from exposing their children to those we are just casually dating as we know that children are subject to building expectations and fears when their parents make any types of changes, including beginning to date.

When we are finding ourselves in need of adult companionship, it is important to shield our children from building these fears and expectations whenever possible. Your children should be left out of your adult social life until such a time that you and your new partner have agreed that you are going to be serious about building a relationship.

It is very tempting to the single parent to include their children in the dating process. A trip to an amusement park or movie theatre may seem harmless enough with that cute date you have been seeing for a few weeks, however, remember that children project your romantic partners into the complimentary parental role. These projections can be positive or negative in nature. If you are unsure in any way as to whether this person will be around next week, it is better to exclude the children. You do not want to place any undue stress on your children nor do you want to build any unrealistic expectations in your children.

Dating openly in front of your impressionable offspring on a casual basis will build a sense of insecurity in your child. How many prospective partners will cycle in and out of your life before their impressionable young eyes? How many will begin to build an attachment to someone you are dating only to have it end abruptly when you break it off?

Before introducing your current love interest to your youngster or teenager, review your own relationship history. Have you made good, solid choices and had longevity in your relationships or have you had a series of brief but heated affairs? If your relationship history falls into the latter category refrain from introducing your children into the situation until you have well established the new relationship no matter how long it may take.

If you are a person who seems to make good choices and your past relationships have been steady and long-lived you can make the introduction once you and your new partner have decided to be mutually exclusive and committed to building a future together. This may take several months. In a healthy situation this decision can usually be reached in the three to six month period after dating commences.

Dependent upon the age of your children, they may well be aware that you are dating someone. Curious children may even ask to meet the individual in question. Unless a true relationship is developing where the party in question is likely to become an integral part of your life and the lives of your children, it is wise to keep the relationships segregated.

What if you meet someone while your children are with you and then begin to date or begin dating someone whom your children are acquainted with like a baseball coach or youth leader? The same rules apply. Until you are certain that you are going to be in an ongoing relationship with the person in question, keep the relationships separate.

If you allow your children to meet a person or persons that move in and out of your life on a frequent basis you are going to create a sense of insecurity in your child. It is human nature to try to make an impression on the children of someone you are interested in romantically. You do not want anyone to have the power to make an impression on your children from the projected position of your "partner" unless they are going to be an integral part of your life. Children do not need to be exposed to anyone you are dating until you are relatively certain that they are on the way to becoming your significant other, otherwise, they are insignificant to your children.

What Do You Need to be Happy?

What is it that you require in order to be happy?

Are you already happy and not in need of anything in particular? Good for you! You probably are one of the people who will not read this blog, so I will address those that feel that something is missing in their quality of life preventing them from being contented *(happy).*

Is it financial safety and security?

Many of us in these difficult economic times are back down at the bottom of the Maslow Pyramid hierarchy of needs. At the safety level, we require security of body, employment, resources, morality, safety of the family, of our health and of our property.

This is not unusual, when the economy takes a downturn, I would venture to guess that at the closure of 2009 the majority of us know of someone who is dealing with the threat of foreclosure, may be considering taking our children out of private schools, and is concerned about job security.

It is difficult indeed to be happy when basic survival and quality of life is at risk.

We can take control over these security risks to some degree, we can search for a new type of employment, downsize our home, refinance, but it is difficult. These factors lay a foundation for the balance of our energy and when these foundational building blocks of our lives begin to shift, we may feel it in all areas of our life.

It is difficult to maintain optimism during these times, but it is possible. We do as much as we can to cement our foundations and we give thanks for the positives that still remain, we weather the storm and prepare for standing our ground or possibly rebuilding.

The Dating Game

Our spirituality may help us to endure difficult times at this level and may restore us on the emotional level but we are at risk for depression and high anxiety and must stay aware that life runs in cycles and that this cycle too will pass.

Perhaps you are feeling that you are okay at the safety and security level, a little nervous, but not being affected too harshly, in that case you are probably feeling more that you need love and a sense of belonging to be happy.

Do you need to feel loved and to feel a sense of belonging?

I would venture to say that eighty percent of the clients I am working with are at this level of Maslow's hierarchy of needs.

Feeling love and partnership, (*belonging*), would bring the majority of the seekers I speak with a sense of happiness.

At this level we seek friendship, family and sexual intimacy.

We may find that in finding sexual intimacy we are falling short of that feeling of happiness we seek. It may be simple enough to find willing sexual partners, but not so easy to find that combination of friendship and sexual intimacy that is the foundation of what we commonly refer to as love.

How do we improve our chances of finding a fulfilling relationship?

It is not easy.

We must learn to differentiate love and sex.

Sex is chemical and can lay a firm foundation for love, but friendship is psychological and emotional and is truly the cement that holds a sexually charged partnership together.

The Dating Game

Sexual chemistry can be immediate, like a thunderbolt, whereas friendship, although at times immediate, usually takes patience and understanding, taking the time to get to know someone.

When we delay our sexual gratification and take the time to truly get to understand another person on a "*friendship*" level and create that bond of affection and concern we have a much better chance at finding our happiness at this level.

There is no magic formula, no rule of thumb for how long it takes, but history and experience prove that the more you know someone before handing your heart over to them, the higher your chances of success in forging that bond we refer to as love.

Perhaps we feel we have already met our love but we are having difficulty transitioning from friendship or casual sex to true intimacy?

If that is the case, the best thing to do is to move things back to the ground level, remove the sexual activity and focus on the friendship again, you may or may not get to the level of sexual intimacy you desire, but you will be able to see things in a broader perspective. Letting go frequently allows the sexual chemistry to reignite into a more passionate connection, yes, it may not, but it frees you to seek the love you desire elsewhere rather than treading water in a "*friends with benefits*" situation. If love is what you seek, *a friend with benefits is only a purgatory that you confine yourself to.*

Perhaps we feel that we have met our love but have lost them and feel that only in regaining this love can we find true happiness?

At times, we have found the love we need and for whatever reason, something has gone wrong and we no longer have that love in our lives. How much energy should we put into regaining that love?

This is one of the most difficult situations to calculate.

The Dating Game

Each situation is different, however, in general, if initial direct attempts at reconciliation fail, it is best to accept the loss and move forward as best as one can. The old adage, **"absence makes the heart grow fonder"** holds true here. If the love is meant to rekindle, you cannot force it, nor should you put your life on hold waiting for it, you must accept the ending as a clean break and begin to move forward with your life.

Truly, you can find happiness elsewhere, there is no one person who defines whether or not you are happy, you, yourself define whether or not you are content. In holding on and hoping for a lovers' return you are losing opportunities for new love to enter your life, that can, actually, make you happy.

The best practice is to move forward. Your lover may return. When and if that love does resurface should not be the sole factor in whether or not you are happy. It is not healthy.

In moving forward, we frequently find a new love that is better for us psychologically and emotionally because that lover allows themselves to be available to us, the key to intimacy.

When a desired love object is not available to us emotionally, psychologically or physically we are dealing with the extreme opposite of intimacy, seclusion, and this is something that we are incapable of changing, it must come from within the other person.

If we have love and safety, we may well feel that a heightened sense of esteem will bring us happiness.

Will esteem make you happy?

Do you want to be respected, do you have a high sense of self-esteem, do you want broader recognition of your achievements?

If so, then you are higher up on the pyramid, you have a firm foundation of security and love and you are ready to receive the acclaim of your fellow man. You will work hard to achieve your goals and gain continued recognition and this will make you happy.

Hard work and fortitude is likely what is needed to bring you to your happy plateau.

Are you ready to self-actualize?

If you are, you are truly on "**top of the heap**". In Maslow's theory, this is where true happiness can be found, your physiological, psychological, emotional and ego-driven needs have all been met. You are ready to be the best you can be, and this will bring you true happiness of the highest sort.

At this point you can be creative, helpful, nonjudgmental, charitable and accepting.

You are ready to help others to achieve their happiness as well.

So, where are you on Maslow's pyramid? What do you need to be happy? What can you do to achieve your goals?